280.1

W9-AGX-943

AND YET IT MOVES

KANSAS SCHOOL OF RELIGION
UNIVERSITY OF KANSAS
1300 OREAD AVENUE
LAWRENCE, KANSAS 66044

BX 8.2
.L 28513

AND YET IT MOVES

Dream and reality of the ecumenical movement

By

ERNST LANGE

Translated by Edwin Robertson

CHRISTIAN JOURNALS LIMITED
Belfast, Dublin, Ottawa
THE WORLD COUNCIL OF CHURCHES
Geneva

Original title: Die ökumenische Utopie oder Was bewegt die ökumenische Bewegung?
© Kreuz Verlag, Stuttgart, FRG.

English edition, abridged by Dr. Konrad Raiser and Dr. Lukas Vischer

English edition 1979 by Christian Journals Limited, 2 Bristow Park, Belfast, BT9 6TH and 760 Somerset Street W, Ottawa, Ont., Canada and World Council of Churches, Geneva.

Copyright © Christian Journals Limited 1978.

All rights reserved. This book is sold subject to the conditions that it shall not, by way of trade or otherwise, be lent, re-sold, hired out or otherwise circulated without the publishers' prior consent to any form of binding or cover other than in which it is published and without a similar condition including this condition being imposed on the subsequent purchase. No part of this publication may be reproduced, stored in a retrieval system, or transmitted, in any form or by any means, electronic, mechanical, photocopying, recording or otherwise, without the prior permission of the publishers.

World Council of Churches
Ecumenical movement

Cover design: N Witte—Brooymans.

CJL   ISBN 0 904302 48 2
WCC ISBN 2 8254 0601 5

Made and printed in Ireland.

Table of Contents

Introduction

I am delighted that this book should now at last be appearing in an English translation. I consider it one of the most perceptive and impressive interpretations of the ecumenical movement and its problems. The occasion of its writing was a particular ecumenical conference. I had invited Ernst Lange to attend the Faith and Order Commission meeting in Louvaiñ in 1971 and subsequently to write an account of it. But the report which Lange produced far exceeded my expectations. While it certainly provided an account and analysis of this conference in all its facets, Lange used the opportunity afforded by his assignment to present at the same time a study of the whole Faith and Order movement and its problems. Indeed, the book became so to speak a presentation of Lange's own interpretation of the ecumenical movement and a distillation of all the rich experience of his Geneva years.

The reader of this book will have no difficulty in imagining how stimulating and enriching personal contact with Ernst Lange could be. He was one of those colleagues who constantly reflect on the work of the World Council of Churches and seek to understand its significance more clearly. He was an exacting colleague who would raise questions where none were visible to others. This was why discussions with him so often led to unexpected and surprising results.

I do not find it easy to describe him. Perhaps the best way will be to recall two conversations with him which were especially important to me personally.

We first met during his initial visit to Geneva. He asked detailed questions concerning the work and organization of the World Council. Then he tried to explain what it was that

1

specially concerned him and in this connection asked me:
'What do you think of preaching? What can be done here to
revitalize preaching?' I have often thought about this question
since. Ernst Lange had a very special concern with the
preaching of the Gospel. In this respect he was, in his own
words, 'a committed Protestant'. He had great skill in
analysing biblical texts. But, for him, analysis was not
enough. His deepest concern was that the texts should speak.
How do we bridge the gap between a merely intellectual
understanding and description of a biblical text and the
proclamation of the Gospel? This was the problem from
which he found it impossible to escape. I say 'escape', for it
was patent that he did not find preaching easy. The pregnant
formulations so characteristic of his style did not come
effortlessly to him. He had to wrestle not only in order to
understand but also, and above all, to find the right words.
The difficulty of saying something as it needed to be said
could plunge him into a state of inner tension which was
sometimes almost unbearable in its intensity. But then, when
he succeeded in finding just the words he wanted, his eyes
would light up with a smile of relief.

The second conversation was only a few weeks before he
died. He was on a short visit to Geneva. He and some friends
were planning to publish a book about the Church. He
himself had recently completed a sociological study of the
Evangelical Church in Germany in the course of which he
once again observed how little the life of the Church as really
lived and experienced by its members can be captured in
theological terms. 'The members have quite different
responses and expectations.' The question he wanted to
explore was how real renewal could come to the Church. He
wanted me to contribute a chapter on 'the way the ecumenical
movement moralizes the Church'. By this he meant that the
call to renewal and unity had the almost inevitable effect not
of liberating the Church but of smothering it with new
demands and obligations. 'But what I want to know is how
the discovery of our universal fellowship can be an experience
of real liberation.' This project reflected a concern which was
never absent from his thinking. How is real fellowship to be
achieved? He realized that the Gospel is only the Gospel when
it establishes fellowship and, conversely, that fellowship is

only fellowship when it is established by the Gospel. This explains his intense interest in the transition from proclamation to fellowship.

These two conversations seem to me to illustrate qualities which. also characterize .Lange's report of the Louvain conference.

In the first place, the book displays Ernst Lange's remarkable gifts as an interpreter. His account of the conference is painstaking and faithful. He analyses each text and seeks to interpret it in its context in the discussion. Conference texts seldom if ever rank as great literature. Yet Ernst Lange does not shrink from probing every detail. And the miracle is that he makes these texts speak with an eloquence they could never achieve unaided. Whereas others who read them have to prod themselves to read on, he finds statements which are 'exciting' and even 'explosive'. He has a keen eye for the places where promising developments are foreshadowed. A tiny surface hint is sufficient to enable him to describe the whole plant which could eventually grow from it. Those who actually took part in the Louvain meeting will find Lange's interpretation a particularly outstanding achievement. They will discover aspects and depths which were previously hidden from them.

But, above all, Lange's account is sustained by a passionate concern that the ecumenical movement should achieve its goal. This concern may not be immediately obvious to every reader, for Lange subjects the ecumenical movement to such a rigorous critical analysis that the reader may at first see only the problematic aspects of the great quest for unity. But the critical portrait of this quest is basically a summons to the churches to move beyond the present situation of neither one thing nor the other, neither separation nor unity. He recognizes the danger that the churches may only 'play' with the possibility of unity. 'Play is splendid. Play is a vital part of life. But we can spend too much time in play. We can gamble away our opportunity.' Lange recognizes the danger of the churches' despairing of their task and retreating from the world. Yet their presence is needed in the world today more than ever before. They must therefore rediscover their task and carry it out. But in a world in which peace and survival are at risk, they can only do this if they move forward resolutely into unity. In the last analysis, Ernst Lange's report is essentially an attempt to make us realize the urgency of this summons.

Lukas Vischer

The First Letter

The Vulnerability of Ecumenical Commitment

Dear Friend,

I have made an ecumenical trip on your behalf. At least, I have tried to. That will astonish you, for when we last met, quite by chance, on the main railway station in Frankfurt, you made it quite clear to me that you were no longer interested in Christianity or in its future — the ecumenical movement.

You made your own the famous saying of the young Karl Marx: 'For me the criticism of religion is essentially complete'.[1] But your Christianity had always been a gesture of protest. That was why you were interested in the ecumenical movement for quite some time. You saw this movement as the most massive domestic Christian protest against the way Christianity, by its alliance with the powers that be, had been transformed into its exact opposite. But then you became more and more convinced that the ecumenical protest was no more successful in dealing with the poverty of Christianity than it was in dealing with the poverty of mankind. In the last analysis, it was itself simply an 'expression', a reflection of this double poverty, at world level. In any case, your mind was already made up. For you the poverty of mankind was far more important than the poverty of Christianity. And if you had to give your dream a name, you at any rate preferred the Marxist *Internationale* to the Christian Ecumenical Movement!

All that was perfectly clear. Then what right had I to saddle you with the responsibility for my ecumenical trip? Let me try to explain.

I

We first became acquainted with each other in 1960, at the
European Ecumenical Youth Conference in Lausanne, you
remember.[2] At that time you were a second year theological
student and I was still quite a young parson. The main
characteristic we shared was our impatience. It was in
Lausanne that we first heard the slogans which were to
dominate the ecumenical scene in the sixties: 'world
development', 'grass-roots ecumenism', and 'revolution'.
Perhaps for the first time in an ecumenical setting, we saw the
world in a new and shocking light: a world divided, not so
much between East and West as we had so long believed but
between North and South, between the 'haves' and the 'have-
nots'. There was a 'third' world, the world of those who were
still being exploited as they always had been exploited. We
asked what this shadow world meant, for the white, rich and
powerful countries and churches. Geneva 1966[3] was still a
long way off. We did not yet have the language to express
what we felt to be imminent: a situation in which civil war on
a world scale threatened, indeed was already flaring up in
places, a world of two, three, many Vietnams. And we began
to feel ashamed of our complacency as churches, our
disregard of the world.

We were excited by the effortlessness of the ecumenical
accord which the conference daily demonstrated to us, yet at
the same time disturbed by it. We were certainly not united
but we did undoubtedly feel a sense of solidarity deeper than
the national and confessional boundaries, stronger even than
the Iron Curtain itself. But how relevant and how important
was this solidarity? Even the possibility that this kind of
ecumenical activity with its free-ranging rootlessness might
turn out to be beside the point made us feel helpless and
restless. We wanted to change the churches ecumenically,
root and branch, especially the local churches to which we
had to return. Here too, the language in which to express all
this had still to be invented. It was in New Delhi in 1961[4] that
we were first given the formula 'all in each place' but at least
we felt the problem. Nor were we only concerned with
everyday ecumenism in the local church. The question we
wanted to probe was: What difference does the ecumenical

movement make? What does it really change? And so it was that into this tension between our new and disturbing awareness of the world and our impatient longing to discover an ecumenical *praxis,* the ominous word 'revolution' was dropped, a word which Christianity has not been able to dispense with since, because the world in which it lives and for which it proposes to live finds it indispensable. 'The revolutionaries have left us already!', complained Hans Hoekendijk.[5] He meant revolutionary in a general sense, leading to renewal, radical reform. Above all, he meant the spirit of revolt. He mourns the loss of a radicalized youth movement in the churches, a protest against the fathers. He certainly did not want parricide, involving revolution in the sense of the violent overthrow of oppression at all costs. But words are 'loaded pistols', at least when they verbalize undefined obligations left hanging in the air. In a pre-revolutionary world situation even vague talk of revolution is explosive. It makes visible a possibility, points to an alternative. Since Lausanne — and at the beginning of the sixties there were of course many Lausannes — the fuse had been lit, even for the younger generation in the churches.

It was also on this point that we had our first argument. As you will remember, it concerned something which at first sight has nothing whatever to do with revolution, the subject of intercommunion. In company with many of the conference members, you were in the mood to force the official churches to advance ecumenically by staging a united act of collective disobedience. You wanted the Conference — in defiance of all ecumenical protocol — to celebrate a united eucharist and to invite everyone, even the Orthodox, even the young Swiss Catholic observers. Surely we were one, surely we belonged together across all the barriers! What right had the bishops and church authorities to forbid us to celebrate this unity, from setting the seal on it?

I was older than you and, besides, had an official role in the Conference. In other words, I was in a sense part of the 'establishment' which you wanted to put under pressure in order to force it to act. So I tried to persuade you that it was wrong to precipitate conflict, wrong to endanger the consensus already achieved. I still recall the argument I used. This was the most significant renewal movement of this century, not only for the churches but even for the world. This movement was the work of the Spirit. This was not something to be jeopardized. Challenge was good but violent solutions are bad because they destroy the basis of dialogue.

I don't think I convinced you. In any event both of us were only on the fringe of what was happening. In any case, at that time it was still fairly easy for the 'establishment' to get its way despite pressure from below. There was a compromise. A united communion service was held, but outside the official conference programme and only in the form of an 'open communion' at the invitation of fourteen pastors. Many came to it, but the whole thing was never anything more than a largely Protestant, semi-private occasion. The revolution had not taken place.

II

I know that since Lausanne our ways have diverged increasingly. We have profited from our experience in quite different ways.

Your catchwords have been 'world development' and 'revolution'. They led you further towards the 'left'. Shortly after Lausanne you abandoned your theological studies and turned to political science. You began to study Marx. You found your niche in the Socialist Student Association, though at first still keeping up your gesture of Christian protest. Then came the disturbances in the universities. At the time you were already reading for your doctorate. At the Berlin demonstration against the visit of the Shah of Persia you had your first taste of the rubber-truncheon. We heard your name mentioned in discussions about the strategy of protest: violence against property, violence against persons, work with marginal groups, the long march through the institutions. You quickly took the measure of the temptation to anarchism. Today you are a man of the radical left among the Young Socialists, an embarrassment to our political Christians. Your language has become very inflexible and esoteric. I understand your intensity better. You realize that the classic revolution is now no longer possible here in Germany. The capacity of neo-capitalism to unify is as notorious as its

incapacity to hold off world-destruction, which it goes on
producing and exporting to the ends of the earth. So your
strategy is the struggle for political power at the grass-roots,
education for liberation, reforms which break the system,
permanent revolution.

My own catchwords have been 'grass-roots ecumenism',
'church reform'. For me and my friends the period of church
experiments began, the testing of alternative forms of church
life and action. We, too, became increasingly radical in our
thought and action, especially when we noticed that our
strenuous search for the Church of the future was dismissed as
uncomfortable but harmless charismatic exuberance. We
learned that structures are not changed by arguments but
only by the pressure of a changed public opinion. We learned
to live with conflicts, to court the risk of conflicts, to 'stage'
conflicts, in order to produce this change. We learned to
assess organized religion more realistically, to see it as a
constant compromise between social needs, the concern of
institutions with self-preservation, and the promptings of the
Gospel promise. But we remained quite deliberately within
the Church, despite our growing and vigorous concern with
world problems. We kept firm hold of the ecumenical utopia,
the utopian dream of a united and renewed Christendom
which would be the 'leaven', the pattern, the stimulus of the
coming world community, the custodian of a source of
humanization which is not only inexhaustible but also always
far in advance of every form of human achievement yet
realized in history, namely, the humanity of Jesus of
Nazareth. We held on to this utopia because it seemed
concrete enough to be the basis of praxis and open enough to
keep hope bright and prevent us from resignation in our
praxis. We tested theologies, strategies, programmes,
discarding them again when they proved inadequate to our
vision and our hope. But we clung firmly to the Pentecostal
promise.

Occasionally we exchanged letters, you and I. We sent each
other working papers and assured each other of our
continuing understanding and sympathy, but across a
widening gulf. I remember sending you a poem by Rudolf
Otto Wiemer entitled 'Sketch for an Easter Hymn' because it
expressed — and still expresses today — in an incomparable

way my own hopes. You responded, I remember, with
Brecht's 'Spring 1938'. I got your message: this is still
Passiontide and not yet Easter.

In your covering letter you told me you had decided to
accept the radical consequences of christology. God has
become man again. From now on we must hold man in
reverence.

III

At the end of the sixties, my uneasiness grew. I was now in
Geneva with the World Council of Churches. In a real sense I
was at home, for this ecumenical movement was my 'native
heath', its goal my 'promised land'.

My uneasiness was not due to any disappointment with the
work in Geneva. The day to day administration of ecumenical
work is just as demanding, just as packed with new
experiences, new opportunities to grow in knowledge and
capacity, as the ecumenical festivals, the great international
conferences.

But no one can do ecumenical work without suffering
increasingly under the three great crosses of the ecumenical
movement.

First there is the cross of the growing credibility gap. In the
sixty years since Edinburgh, an extraordinarily impressive
and largely convincing consensus has been achieved: a
consensus in awareness of the problems, a consensus in
convictions and aims. But it is a verbal consensus. Except in
the area of Christian service this verbal consensus issues in
hardly any praxis worth speaking of. It isn't a question of
goodwill. But the constitution of the World Council of
Churches has been so devised that the Council simply cannot
take action. It is a movement of the *churches*. And the churches
have limited its field of activity. What they want is a
consultative forum, not an instrument to make decisions and
implement them. But a consensus consisting of words of no
consequence is perilous and daily becomes more so.
Kierkegaard's parable of the geese is a definitive statement of
this truth.

The action appropriate to the verbal consensus lies with the churches. And this brings me to the second cross, that of a twofold impotence. On the one hand, the World Council has no authority to compel the churches to act. In William Temple's oft-quoted words, the only power the Council has is the 'wisdom of its arguments'. On the other hand, the churches, which have the power, have great difficulty in exercising it at the ecumenical level. For this power rests on the structured piety of their members, which is thoroughly parochial in character, giving legitimacy and stability to the particular rather than to the universal dimension, to the individual conscience, the small group, the local community.

And here is where the third cross appears. The only way in which the verbal consensus can be matched by the appropriate praxis is for the church members to be delivered from their imprisonment in a parochial outlook. Only if the universal dimension of human existence in the contemporary world can be really firmly implanted in the daily *praxis pietatis* of church members, and thus bring about a change in public opinion in the churches, will it become possible for the churches really to apply their power at the ecumenical level and for the World Council of Churches to be made capable of effective action. But, even if it were not forbidden, it would not even be possible for the ecumenical movement to exercise direct influence on the church members. The distance separating the churches at the ground level of the local congregations from the decision-making bodies at the international level — the level of official ecumenical action — is astronomic.

Does this mean that the ecumenical game must remain merely a word-game? This question was all the more disquieting in view of the fact that you, with your strategy, were not merely discussing changes but actually effecting them, that you were actually bringing to bear on the institutions, on the universities, the schools, the parties, the unions, the kind of pressure of which we only dreamed. You were creating the climate of opinion in which at least the possibility of change and the necessity for change were beginning to lodge in the public consciousness. Even where your protest failed, its very 'failure' seemed far more successful than the ecumenical movement's 'success', which increased visibly year by year.

Shortly afterwards I left Geneva. Not because of this disquiet but for other reasons. Yet my disquiet has grown since then. What relevance, what importance, does the ecumenical consensus have? What capacity to renew church and society? What moves the ecumenical movement and what does it affect?

I had been invited to attend the meeting of the Faith and Order Commission in the Belgian university town of Louvain in August 1971 and to write a critical report of it. On my way to Louvain I ran into you, quite by chance, and told you of my plans. I was delighted to be going to Louvain and my delight must have been quite obvious. With the rather brutal frankness which clearly is part and parcel of your style of rebellion, you told me you thought ecumenical journeys a waste of time.

That went home! And, sitting in the train afterwards, on my way to Belgium, I decided to make this the starting point for my observations in Louvain. Was the ecumenical journey a waste of time? Was it ultimately even a waste of time for me and my friends? I wanted to view what happened at Louvain, as far as possible, through your eyes, the eyes of one who keeps his distance. Of course I am, and in one way or other will always remain, an ecumenist. As I've already said, the ecumenical movement is my home. But sometimes the home one loves can become a strange place. Sometimes we even have to leave home, just because it is hemming us in.

I attach some notes I made for my own use, some of the thoughts that occurred to me. I don't yet know what conclusions I have to draw from them. But I don't think I wasted my time! I look forward very much to your reactions.

Friendly greetings,

E.L.

The Parable of the Geese

Supposing wild geese could speak? Then they would arrange their own church services.

They would come together on Sundays and a gander would preach the sermon. The burden of his sermon would be: what a lofty destiny geese have! What a sublime goal the Creator (and whenever His Name was uttered the geese would curtsey and the ganders would bow their heads) had set before them. With the aid of their wings they would be able to fly off to distant lands, to blessed climes where they would really feel at home, for here they were only strangers.

So it would happen every Sunday. And as soon as they came out of church they would waddle off home to their own affairs. And then off to church the next Sunday and then home again. And that was the end of it; they prospered and looked good, became plump and tender . . . and then at Christmas they were served up and eaten. And that was the end of it. That was the end of it. For though the sermon on Sunday had sounded wonderful, on Monday the geese would be busily telling each other what would happen to a goose that really wanted to use the wings the Creator had provided and destined for the high goal set before it, what would befall it, what an awful fate would overtake it. This was one subject on which the geese were quite unanimous. But of course, it would have been unseemly to speak of this on Sundays. For, as they said, it would then become obvious that our divine service is really only making a fool of God and of ourselves.

Among the geese, however, there were one or two individuals who seemed to be suffering and these remained thin and scraggy. The other geese would talk about them and say: 'There, you see what comes of taking this flying business so seriously! It's because their hearts are so full of the desire

13

fly that they become so thin, do not thrive, do not have the grace of God as we do, which is why we are so plump and tender. And so they would go again to church the next Sunday and the old gander would preach about the sublime goal the Creator (and here again the geese would curtsey and the ganders bow their head) had set before geese and given them wings specially for this purpose.

Soren Kierkegaard[6]

The Strange World of the Ecumenical Movement

Dear Friend,

In whatever part of the world they are held, ecumenical conferences are like Hilton Hotels, as alike as peas in a pod. The distinctive scenery is there only as background, the stage setting, somewhere to escape into in your free time. But there isn't much free time. In any part of the world, the ecumenical movement is noted for industry and hard work, which is not surprising in view of its Anglo-Saxon origins. You work in the evenings and usually on Sundays, too. Occasionally there is a reception or a trip into the surrounding countryside. You see a little local colour then, though mostly through the windows of a bus.

It would hardly be true to say I went to Louvain. I wasn't in Louvain at all. I was at a Faith and Order Conference.[7] It happened to be taking place in the university town of Louvain in Belgium, in the college of the Flemish-speaking Jesuits in Haverlee near Louvain, to be precise.

I

The choice of the theme 'Unity in the Church — Unity of Mankind' for a conference in Louvain, of all places, had a certain irony. For the struggle over languages in Belgium divides people who have lived together for centuries. The Catholic University, founded in 1425, was itself caught up in this conflict. The Flemish-speaking section was still in Louvain but the French-speaking section had moved to a modern set of buildings elsewhere. Even the Jesuit fathers are

15

housed in separate buildings according to language. I spoke
with one of the Flemish fathers about this problem. He
suggested tentatively that this very separation was perhaps a
step towards real unity. For the first time, the university was
no longer troubled by constant disputes over status and
parity. There was a really cooperative and constructive
atmosphere now.

A lesson on the theme of unity. The lost unity had been a
unity of inequality. Flemish was the language of the under-
privileged, mostly the peasants and workers. French was the
language of the upper classes, the property owners, the
educated. Your prospects were brighter if you spoke French.
The conflict over language is very largely a class conflict. The
former unity mainly benefited the upper classes. What is true
in the wider area of world conflict between 'whites' and
'blacks', between developing countries and industrial
countries, also holds good for local conflicts. The new unity,
genuine unity, the unity of equality, the unity of those who,
despite their differences, enjoy equal rights, must be
purchased by a redistribution of power, by redressing the
balance of opportunities. And this means dividing those who
are badly joined together because their unity is implicitly
based on violence. It means creating the possibility of
confrontation for the sake of a better unity in the future. How
much of this is also true for the churches?

II

Not only was the Commission the guest of the Catholics. It
was also working for the first time with a group of Roman
Catholic members. This was on the basis of a decision taken
at the Uppsala Assembly in 1968. Although approaches
between Rome and Geneva may seem to be stagnating, there
has been no retreat from the Second Vatican Council. Joint
institutions exist and there is a continuing dialogue. The full
participation of Roman Catholic theologians in Faith and
Order represented a further step, qualitatively, beyond formal
dialogue.

The Commission has a clearly defined mandate, of course.
'To study such questions of faith, order and worship as bear

on this task' (i.e. the task of proclaiming the oneness of the Church) 'and to examine the related social, cultural, political, racial and other factors'.[8] It is a theological forum for discussion and cooperation in matters relating to the unity of the Church. But, like many another agency of the ecumenical movement, it is more *de facto* than it is *de jure*. *De facto* it is one of the most important workshops for ecumenical theology. Theological spring-cleaning is not its only concern. It also works at the achievement of a consensus. In cooperation with other departments of the World Council of Churches, such as Church and Society, it develops the theoretical basis for a world fellowship of churches which, while adhering faithfully to the strategy formulated in Toronto 1950 of not claiming to be a Church in any precise or definable sense, undoubtedly has some ecclesiastical weight. Roman Catholic theologians, officially appointed by the Vatican Secretariat for Unity, are now cooperating in the theological work of the Commission and in its work on the consensus.

The significance of this may be expressed in various ways. When Faith and Order was founded in Geneva in 1920,[9] Charles H. Brent, the spiritual father of the movement, declared: 'I don't think there has been such a representative gathering as this, with the one purpose of doing whatever will make visible the unity of the Church — not since the splitting of the Church centuries ago'.[10] At that time, seventy churches from forty countries were represented. Since then, growth has been swift and continuous. What Brent said at Geneva 1920 was true also of Louvain 1971 in an incomparably fuller measure. Including the representatives of the Roman Catholic Church, the theologians gathered in Louvain represented at least ninety per cent of world Christendom, so far as its religious organizations and its thinking are concerned.

It may also be said that, for the first time in the history of the ecumenical movement, the relative proportions of the churches of Christendom were fairly faithfully reflected in an ecumenical conference. Churches of the 'catholic' type (Orthodoxy, Rome, the Anglican Communion) far out-numbered the 'protestant' wing. Even in Louvain, of course, the numerical proportions were not exact, otherwise the majority of those present should have been representatives of the Roman Catholic Church, and the present rules of the ecumenical numbers game exclude that. All the same, all the major Christian traditions from the Orthodox to the Pentecostalists were for the first time represented and in mutual interplay, on an equal footing and with comparable responsibility.

But statistical triumphalism of this kind is very misleading. In plenary sessions, for example, the Roman Catholic representatives were silent. And it was an ominous silence. Not the silence of 'newcomers' which would have been understandable. Nor a silence betokening lack of interest or involvement. My guess is that it was due to a deep uncertainty.

III

For one thing, no one really knows who represents the Roman Catholic Church today. Belgium is adjacent to Holland. There, too, a relatively stronger, more reformist wind is blowing, one more favourable to the ecumenical movement. But the Vatican Secretariat for Promoting Christian Unity, which appointed the Roman Catholic delegates, is much more cautious in its approach, even though, by comparison with the traditionalist forces in the Vatican, it represents an ecumenical *avant-garde*. When Roman Catholic theologians speak in Faith and Order meetings, whose spokesmen are they? Basically they speak neither for this or that episcopal conference, nor for the Unity Secretariat, nor for the Holy See. They are theologians and, as such, are not official spokesmen of the Church's teaching office and leadership. Within the limits of a considerable academic freedom, they speak for themselves; and, to the extent that they are also somewhat conservatively minded people, they speak with a correspondingly developed sensitivity to the problems involved.

It isn't any different with the other Commission members, of course. They, too, are representatives of their churches only to the extent that the latter have accepted them as nominees of the Assembly of the World Council of Churches. Only to a very limited extent do they speak and contribute to ecumenical studies as official representatives of their churches. They do so only to the extent that they share the consensus in their respective churches and, of course, in the hope that the latter will in turn eventually accept the findings of these studies.

But the Roman Catholic representatives are not accustomed to speaking and working in an open interconfessional forum in this experimental way. Moreover, they find themselves for the first time inside a movement with fifty years' experience behind it. The extent to which the ecumenical consensus has already advanced was more obvious at Louvain than ever before. It now extends even to such central issues as Scripture and Tradition, Ministry and Sacraments. How does Rome view this consensus? How were these Roman Catholic theologians to respond to it now that they could speak as full members of the Commission? Were they to accept it, despite its not being formulated in their language? Or would their very entry into the Commission call it in question once again, in a radical way? Lukas Vischer, the Director of the Faith and Order Secretariat in Geneva, defined this central problem posed by the new representation of the Commission, in the tactful language of ecumenical diplomacy but still very clearly: 'To what extent does it alter the underlying assumptions of our work? What new possibilities exist, now that representatives of the Roman Catholic tradition are actively involved in the Commission's work? Conversely, to what extent does the broader representativeness reopen discussion on agreements already reached? Do we have to reconsider old themes and problems in a new framework?' (*Louvain,* p. 202).

IV

This raises a far deeper question, one which has never really been answered: what is the real value of this ecumenical consensus, if any? We see, on the one hand, a growing pluralism in the individual churches, even in the Roman Catholic Church. On the other hand, we find this lack of clarity about the mandate of the church representatives in ecumenical commissions, and even about the mandate of the ecumenical movement itself. These two problems intensify

each other. And we are left asking naïvely: what does Faith
and Order *do*? What does the ecumenical movement *do*? And
the answer is: they are playing a game — admittedly a very
serious game — with a possibility. The ecumenical movement
— apart from its role as an instrument of international
cooperation — is a workshop in which the future is being
planned, new options worked out for the churches. It is an
anticipation.

Moreover, this game with a possibility, provided it is played
seriously enough and goes on long enough, engenders
something real. It is now quite impossible to return to a pre-
ecumenical age. A member church may decide to quit the
ecumenical organization — as the Dutch Reformed Church of
South Africa did — but no church can in this way escape the
consequences of the ecumenical movement.

This, I believe, explains the silence of the Roman Catholic
representatives in Louvain. Their Church takes words far
more seriously than do the churches of the Word. In certain
conditions words for them are legally binding acts. Even
playing with the possibility of such words raises legal
problems. In fact, when Rome takes a hand in the ecumenical
game, it really ceases to be a game. The other churches leave
the question of authority much more open and so they can
play this game much more lightheartedly, under the
impression that it falls short of a complete commitment on
their part. But *Roma locuta ludus finitus!* When Rome speaks,
the game is over!

V

I sat in a section which gave me a quite new sense of the
oikoumene. You see, in the section meetings, the Roman
Catholic representatives were not silent. Suddenly — it was
also due in part to the subjects under discussion — the
custodians of Protestant theologies found themselves in a clear
minority. Over long stretches, the discussion was between the
Orthodox, the Catholics and the Anglicans. Protestant views
suddenly seemed peripheral. I realized that my reactions to
this were remarkably ambivalent. On the one hand I felt
jubilant that, at long last, the ecumenical movement had

ceased to be a Protestant discussion with a few Orthodox footnotes! At long last, the hitherto 'silent majority' was leading the discussion! On the other hand, I was wondering where this would all lead. Was the Reformation now going to be voted down by a majority?

I then realized that I was suffering from an acoustical illusion. Yes, the majority was speaking — but in English! Sure they were speaking, but as they spoke they were accepting Protestant patterns of speech and thought, a Protestant outlook on the world, a Protestant appreciation of the problems. Moreover, all the speakers were 'frontier workers'. All of them were in breach of the confessional frontier regulations. To a considerable degree, Rome, Constantinople and Moscow had come to terms with, really come to terms with, the Reformation and its heritage. And in the Protestant churches, a first hand or second hand 'catholicism' is steadily gaining ground.

VI

Nevertheless, it becomes more and more puzzling to understand what the WCC Constitution really means by saying (as it has done since Amsterdam 1948) that the ecumenical movement is a movement of the *churches*. The churches are members of the Council but strangely uncommitted members, or at any rate not yet fully committed members. Their representatives on ecumenical bodies have a mandate from the churches but a very loose one. They can say a great deal but it makes very little difference, it achieves very little, officially at any rate. The ecumenical consensus is not inconsiderable but it is written in the future tense and in the subjunctive mood. Although the movement represents something in the region of a thousand million Christians, all its breakthroughs depend on the commitment and inventiveness of a handful of charismatic leaders.

The ecumenical movement is a sort of daydream indulged in by the few on behalf of the many. For the moment, no one can tell whether it will prove in the end to have been a true dream or only an illusion.

It has undeniably had incalculable consequences all over

the world. Even if no one talks about it today, the ecumenical
dream has probably saved the lives of thousands, sheltered
millions of refugees, healed the sick even in the depths of the
jungle, built schools and universities, helped to make peace
negotiations possible. This dream has produced language for
all mankind. Without it, for example, the *Universal Declaration
of Human Rights*[11] — the most important consensus document
of this century — would never have existed. This dream has
also radically transformed many individual Christians and
their organizations, even if in strangely intangible ways. They
think differently, they feel differently, they act differently,
quarrel differently, donate their money differently. Their
scales of values and their priorities have been changed.

This transformation is patent but hardly what caused it. A
few thousand men and women have made journeys, taken
part in ecumenical conferences. Vast libraries have been
written by ecumenists in the last sixty years. They gradually
gather dust and are little consulted. The transforming
element is not to be found in these books, not even in the
volumes on the Faith and Order movement, at least not at
first glance. What is the driving force of the ecumenical
movement? What makes it move?

VII

Worship at an ecumenical conference never fails to be a
painful experience. It is here in worship that a person's
ecumenical experience really begins — the experience of
·joining together in the Lord's Prayer, the undeniable
familiarity of even the most unfamiliar liturgical tradition.
Once we get over the initial shock of unfamiliarity, we know
that the basic shape of the liturgy is the same the world over.
The spirituality of a thousand different forms of Christianity
is nourished from one and the same promise and finds
expression in the same symbols, gestures, rites, needs,
assumptions, sorrows and ecstacies. From the original
patriarchs down to the disciples of Jesus and on through to
the Christian communities of today, wherever they gather,
there is a continuity of religious experience and shared
symbolism.

This makes the liturgical practice of the ecumenical

movement more and more intolerable. Interconfessional
receptions are held and interconfessional visits paid. It is
rather like visiting an exhibition of liturgical history: a room
here full of Byzantine ikons, another containing the
unfinished works of reformist catholicism, and finally, a large
vestibule housing the treasures of evangelical piety,
impossible to catalogue systematically and always giving the
impression of having been arranged any old how. And there
are always certain omissions, involuntary or deliberate.
Despite endless and almost mutually exclusive differen-
tiations, we are united in a *continuum* of spirituality, but
the fellowship actually achieved in ecumenical gatherings
is that of an aestheticizing pseudo-participation by the round-
about way of our capacity for historical empathy.

VIII

We go to a celebration of the Orthodox Liturgy, mercifully
abbreviated to cater to limited Protestant powers of
concentration. One becomes exasperated at the nineteenth
century male-voice tradition which is so out of keeping with
the classic liturgy of the ancient Church, tries with some
difficulty to find one's way in the duplicated text in order to
follow intelligently at least a little of what is going on, and is
delighted when, at the end of the service, the 'bread of the
poor' is distributed to the outsiders — a sort of back-door
intercommunion!

For days an exciting rumour goes the rounds that the
reformist-minded Cardinal is going to find some way of
opening the Sunday Mass to all. While not quite clear as to
how this could possibly be done, one still hopes, because one
still looks for the breakthrough.

But, of course, the open Mass does not in fact materialize.
The eucharistic theology constantly and increasingly invoked
in the ecumenical movement unites all things: heaven and
earth, past and present, our temporal and eternal future, the
spiritual and the material, the human heart and the cosmos,
but, alas, step-brothers are for the present still excluded.

My solitary eucharistic experience in Louvain, apart from
those not included in the official programme, was the evening
meal after the conference ended. The meal was accompanied

by readings, hymns and prayers. But it was not these that
made the meal for me an experience of accomplished
reconciliation, of at-one-ness across all barriers. It was the
fact that I sat beside a clergyman from India, a very dark and
very gentle person. He told me the story of 'Yudhishthira's
Final Trial', taken from the Mahabharata, and how this holy
man refused to enter Paradise because it meant leaving his
beloved dog behind. An instructive tale, though not a
Christian one. It has always seemed to me that the religious
traditions of Asia have the edge over the Christian tradition in
one respect at least — their solidarity does not stop short at
humankind but regards even the animals as brother creatures.

IX

An odd world — this ecumenical world. No doubt it
occasionally has its attractive aspects and can sometimes
kindle enthusiasm. Anyone who has ever attended the
conferences of the UN or its associated agencies knows that
the difference is like that between day and night. Strangely
enough, in the United Nations, the real world, the world of
daily life, is much more remote and fellowship is infinitely
more difficult to achieve. International law may take
precedence over national law, in theory at least. But in
practice, for the most part, the fetish of national sovereignty
effectively bars the way to any real, strong international
solidarity capable of establishing and implementing justice.
In actual fact, the United Nations Organization is not yet a
'community of nations' but merely a multilateral system of
controlled rivalries. As Kohnstamm said,[12] it is still more like
a jungle where the nations circle around each other like
nervous and aggressive wild beasts, even though there may be
efforts to control the traffic on minor side roads.

In the case of the churches the situation is quite the reverse.
The ecumenical movement is confronted with a different
problem from that which confronts the nations. The problem
of the nations is to breathe life into printed rules and already
existing institutions. The problem for the ecumenical
movement, on the contrary, is that it has so far not found the
courage and strength to institutionalize seriously and
committedly the transconfessional and transnational

solidarity which already exists in practice. Ecumenical meetings are far more like international scientific congresses than UN conferences. But they offer even greater possibilities of establishing contact than do scientific congresses. 'Brotherhood' is more than collegial solidarity.

Ecumenists have divided hearts. Insofar as their hearts are in the ecumenical movement, they are astonished and disturbed by the resistance offered by the world to their ecumenical efforts. Insofar as their hearts are claimed by their homes, they are astonished at the remoteness of the ecumenical process from their world. The ecumenical version of this twofold problem of relevance is felt differently and more keenly than it usually is in the daily life of the ordinary Christian, even though he, too, is in fact constantly wrestling with the same question, namely, whether or not he is still the same person on his way into church and on his way home from church. For, every day of his life, the Christian experiences, on the one hand, the alienating power of sin, and, on the other hand, the absence of contemporaneity between his life, thought and speech in the Church and his life, thought and speech in the secular world. Both experiences are painful, but he has already reckoned with this as an inseparable part of his life as a Christian.

But the strangeness of ecumenical experience is another, third aspect. The ecumenical movement is an anticipation of the future of Christendom. What torments us here is the old problem of how to connect the end and the beginning. How can the ecumental beginning be in practice connected with the end of parochial Christianity? How can all this be interlocked so that action becomes possible? For the ecumenical future is certainly not the eschatological future of Christendom. If it were, the connecting of end and beginning would present an insoluble, a purely eschatological problem, i.e. a problem which only God can solve. But it just has to be possible to be connected with this ecumenical future, otherwise it is not my future.

Greetings from one who for the moment is still astonished!

Yours,

E.L.

Chapter One

And Yet It Does Move

or *The Anatomy of the Ecumenical Consensus*

1. The Strategy

According to an early ecumenical slogan: 'Doctrine divides: service unites'. A good deal of clever ecumenical strategy lay behind this neat formula.

Modern ecumenism is a breakthrough of the Holy Spirit, a purely religious awakening, but it did not come into existence independently of social conditions. The missionary movement of the nineteenth century, the greatest in Christian history, was fatally allied to the colonialism and imperialism of the North Atlantic industrial nations, even though it certainly cannot be written off simply as a religious epiphenomenon of this political and economic conquest of the world.

This alliance was increasingly at odds with the broadly conceived aim of missions. If the 'whole world' was to be evangelized 'in *one* generation', as people caught up in the enthusiasm generated by the student revival at the end of the nineteenth century dared to hope, then the national versions of Christianity in Europe and North America[13] would have to think of others besides themselves, at least in their missionary work. They would have to live down their reputation of being mere stooges of white lust for world conquest. The need to do so became all the more pressing as unrest grew among the conquered peoples. The individual Christian traditions would have to acquire a new respect for the primitive universality of Christianity. Only in this way would real indigenization be

27

achieved and Christianity put down firm roots in all parts of the world, in all languages and cultures. Only in this way would it be possible to distinguish between evangelization and imperialism. Only in this way would evangelism keep its credibility. Only in this way could missionaries build on enduring and healthy foundations in their service, in their educational and medical work, in their plans for developing community and building up the Church, in their development aid, in their work of consciousness-raising.

Moreover, even the professional propagandists and fund-raisers for missions faced an exceptionally difficult task. How little power missions had, how weak and alone and poor the individual missionary was in the big wide world, became especially obvious when they tried to dissociate themselves from their colonialist allies. The cynical export of confessional quarrels and divisions from the 'sending' countries, the unholy rivalry and competition between missionaries — all this was simply wasteful and uneconomic — quite apart from its erosion of credibility. To anyone thinking ahead and strategically, the immediate need was cooperation on the mission field, at least a minimum of agreement, comity and mutual support.

A further complication was that, at the very moment when Christianity was succeeding at the world level, it was rapidly losing its home base. The process of secularization went steadily forward and its pace even quickened. It was no longer possible to turn a blind eye to the retreat from the Church and from Christianity on the part of great masses of the people in traditionally Christian societies, even if opinions differed as to its causes, extent and significance. The alliance between Christianity and society, which even in the mission field seemed increasingly questionable on practical grounds alone, was rapidly melting away even in the home countries of the 'mother churches'. The trend to a greater self-reliance and mutual cooperation on the part of the churches in both situations seemed inevitable.

The terrible shock administered by the outbreak of the First World War dispelled any lingering doubts about this. For the churches discovered that their traditional alliances with national states and cultures and with particular groups in their particular societies made them quite incapable of achieving anything for peace or staving off the menace of disaster on a world scale. They were so captive to traditional solidarities that they were not even able to resist the war propaganda of their respective countries. The Triune God had been exchanged for an Olympus of warring tribal gods.[14]

Cooperation was in the air, therefore. Despite Christendom's thousand years of increasing fragmentation, the ecumenical imperative had never been completely silenced, rooted as it is in the very foundations of the tradition of Christian faith; but now it became peremptory, brooking no denial.

But *how* were the churches to find fellowship with one another? The pioneers of the world missionary movement and the 'life and work' movement put their confidence in the unifying power of practical love, in the diaconal motive in the widest sense. For they knew, or thought they knew, that 'doctrine divides'. It was not that they were pragmatists sceptical of all theorizing, devotees of a more ethically slanted 'practical Christianity', less interested in religious beliefs than in their practical consequences. Unreflective activism of this kind was certainly not characteristic of a man like Nathan Söderblom, for example, who was a leading expert in the history of religion. On the contrary, like most of his fellow pioneers, he was perfectly familiar with the laws governing the development of Christian doctrine and church order. Churches have always defined their doctrine with special reference to the struggle against heresy. The definition of doctrine is itself an act of conflict. And as far as church structures are concerned, these certainly owe their origin at least partly to certain social and cultural conditions in the context in which missionary work and the development of the Church have taken place. And even the structures have only been made a question of principle and given dogmatic status in the struggle with and the defence against schismatic movements. Definitions of doctrine and of church order 'divide' because this is precisely their function. They divide 'those within' from 'those without', those who belong from those who do not. They define a church's own identity by excluding the non-identical. Definitions of doctrine and of order, whatever other functions they may have, *also* have an excommunicative function.

Since the process of division began, the church traditions resulting from it have also been in competition with each other, even where there has been no active proselytism. This applies especially to churches which have accepted the responsibility of providing religious legitimacy and stability to the unity of some nation, society or commonwealth. Any religious alternative then represents a threat to their monopoly and even to the interests of the society which they serve. Even interests of this kind, in competition and self-preservation, find their way into definitions of doctrine and order and, above all, into the history of their development and influence.

Doctrine and order seemed, therefore, not to be an appropriate field for contact, cooperation and the development of fellowship between the churches, at least not at first. They *are* the conflict between the churches, in concentrated verbal form.

This enables us to understand just how daring was the vision of Charles H. Brent, Robert Gardiner and their friends in the pioneer generation of the Faith and Order movement. What they wanted to tackle as their theme was that which divides, whose function it is to divide! As we might put it today, they wanted to uncover the conflict potential of doctrinal formulas and structural forms. They wanted to 'stage' the conflict between the churches and to bring it to a head under controlled conditions. Even the pioneers of the world missionary movement and of the life and work movement wanted cooperation and *more* than cooperation. They, too, wanted the reunion of Christendom. But they worked with a different model of union, a more modest one, one which promised swifter success. Moreover, their personal biographies and temperament led them to consider mission and service to be far more important dimensions of the Church's life than its structural unity.

Contrary to all appearances, the Faith and Order vision was the more radical one and its strategy the bolder one. We are consequently all the more surprised to learn that Brent's 'conversion' had already taken place in Edinburgh in 1910 and that it was only a few months later that he set to work to put his plan into operation. This he did by persuading his own church, the Protestant Episcopal Church, 'to take under advisement the promotion by this Church of a Conference following the general method of the World Missionary Conference, to be participated in by representatives of all Christian bodies throughout the world which accept our Lord Jesus Christ as God and Saviour, for the consideration of questions pertaining to the Faith and Order of the Church of Christ'.[16]

Still more important was the decision about method taken in April 1911 by the Committee set up the previous year. The proposed Conference was to be prepared and summoned 'for the definite purpose of discussing those things on which we differ, in the hope that a better understanding of divergent views of faith and order will result in a deepened desire for reunion and in official action on the part of the separated communions themselves'.[17] This decision has unfortunately been labelled as a decision in favour of the method of 'comparative ecclesiology', which suggests that the Faith and Order pioneers were embarking on a futile esoteric theological 'glass bead game'. What they really had in view was something far more daring and dangerous: namely, the 'staging' of conflict, a real exorcism of the demons of divisions. For demons have to be named if they are to be exorcised.

What distinguished the Faith and Order movement from the other currents in the early days of the twentieth century ecumenical movement was not the difference between theory and practice. Strictly speaking, the world missionary movement and the life and work movement were no more 'practical' than Faith and Order. They, too, were basically study and discussion movements. They, too, wrestled with theories about a common praxis for the churches which they, too, would then largely leave to the churches themselves to put into practice. Nor, on the other hand, was Faith and Order more 'theoretical' than these other movements. Its Commission deals with the praxis of the churches at its most far-reaching and most practical, namely, in their worship, their preaching, their instruction, their organized life. The difference lay rather in the priorities and strategies to be adopted in order to achieve the union and renewal of Christendom which was the ultimate goal of all these movements.

Faith and Order was more directly concerned with the goal

of church unity because its representatives had no confidence
in a praxis, mission and service based on leaving existing
differences permanently out of account, i.e. based on the
permanent acceptance of compromise in respect of the
deepest motives and convictions of the churches. The
movement's strategy was to 'stage' the conflict precisely at the
point where the churches identify and define themselves in
opposition to one another. It is by this priority and this
strategy, and by their effectiveness, by the question whether
and to what extent the movement has stuck to its last and
pressed on with its own special business, that Faith and Order
must primarily be judged.

2. The Negative Consensus

Verbally, the fruit of this Faith and Order strategy is at first
sight something quite ordinary and even monumentally dull
— namely, a negative consensus. Of course, there are also
some positive statements. Yet even these seem to serve a
'negative' purpose. They state what does *not* divide or *no longer*
divides. How breathtaking some of these statements really are
only becomes apparent when we set them against the
backcloth of the history of division and its consequences; a
conflict which has riven asunder human beings, groups,
institutions, the one Christendom, but also the societies in
which they live, often over many centuries, is examined, or
cleared up, or, and this is more usual, it becomes clear that
the battle front has shifted, that the traditional conflict has
consequently lost its contemporary relevance.

The first breakthrough of this kind to demonstrate the
fruitfulness of the Faith and Order strategy occurred at the
Second World Conference of Faith and Order in Edinburgh
in 1937 (cf. *Doc. Hist.*, p. 42 ff.). It was the doctrine of grace
which was in question. This had been a focal point of
controversy between 'Protestant' type churches and 'Catholic'
type churches and even among the Protestant churches
themselves. The doctrine of grace lies at the heart of
soteriology which seeks to defend the completeness of the
work of salvation in Jesus Christ and to oppose any dilution,
dislocation, distortion or domestication of the Gospel. In a
sense, soteriology has been from the very beginning the only
real theme of developing Christian doctrine, the real issue

even in the christological and trinitarian controversies in the
ancient Church.

We must be careful here, of course, not to ride off into
abstract generalities. The question of grace is always at the
same time the question of the means of grace, the role of the
Church, the ministry and the sacraments; in other words, the
role of religious institutions in this mediation process. When
controversy breaks out over the meaning of grace, the issue at
stake is, on the one hand, how we are to do justice both to the
sole sovereignty and power of God *and* to man's freedom, both
to the abysmal depths into which sin has plunged the world
and man *and* to the superior power of the act of redemption, to
the divine initiative in the justification of the sinner *and* to the
process of sanctification initiated by justification in which
man is an active participant from the start, and to do so
without reducing the seriousness and importance of either one
or the other.

On the other hand, the problem is also how the Church as
the mediating agency can best respect the mystery of grace.
By minimizing itself (as Protestant ecclesiology seeks to do) or
by magnifying itself (as 'Catholic' ecclesiologies seek to do) in
virtue of the magnitude of the role entrusted to it? By seeing
itself more on the side of the human recipient or more on the
side of the gracious God? By coming forward as the
representative of waiting humanity or as the sure presence of
the prevenient God? What makes the struggle so difficult and
so endless is precisely the fact that, in struggling for the right
understanding of grace, the Church is struggling — one way
or another — for itself, too. And when it struggles for itself it is
also struggling in the last analysis for soteriology. The themes,
interests and motives are so closely interwoven here that all
theorizing is unsatisfactory and is bound to be so. When the
Church speaks of 'grace', it will always be necessary to ask
whether it really only means itself. And this question will
always prompt the counter-question as to whether those who
ask it, and so play off grace against the Church, are really still
starting from the reality of grace, from its bodiliness and
assured presence, at all.

What Edinburgh had to say on the subject of grace needs to
be seen against this background of controversy. It is true that
Rome, one of the main contestants in the public controversy

over man's salvation, was not present in Edinburgh. What was certainly present, however, was the catholic doctrinal tradition, first of all, in its original form in Orthodoxy, and secondly, in the high church tradition within Anglicanism and Protestantism. If the Edinburgh consensus was certainly not broad enough, it nevertheless included the possibility of being broadened.

The Faith and Order strategy is illustrated particularly in the final paragraph, which deliberately picks up the old emotive phrase, *sola gratia*: 'Some churches', it says, 'set great value on the expression *sola gratia* while others avoid it. The phrase has been the subject of much controversy, but we can all join in the following statement: Our salvation is the gift of God and the fruit of His grace. It is not based on the merit of man, but it has its root and foundation in the forgiveness of sins which God in His grace grants to the sinner whom He receives to sanctify him. We do not, however, hold that the action of the divine grace overrides human freedom and responsibility; rather, it is only as response is made by faith to divine grace that true freedom is achieved. Resistance to the appeal of God's outgoing love spells, not freedom, but bondage, and perfect freedom is found only in complete conformity with the good and acceptable and perfect will of God' (*Doc. Hist.*, p. 42).

In other words, none of the disputants withdrew the traditional formulation of the problem in his own church. Nor was there any suggestion that these formulations would not continue to be controversial. What was possible, however, was to try to express the traditional position in a new way so that it ceased to be exclusive and excommunicative and became inclusive and a basis for fellowship. Certainly this did not mean that the conflict was over. Even if this agreement had been more than that of a few theologians, even if the churches they represented were to accept this new formulation officially, they could, and probably would, still interpret it from the standpoint of their own doctrinal tradition. So the consensus is no more than a bridge formula. But have individuals or groups ever reached agreement other than by means of bridge formulas? In other words, by symbols and statements flexible enough to include a variety of experiences, to reconcile them and to present them in their unity? Are words ever more than bridges which still have to be crossed?

But even that concluding paragraph of the Edinburgh Conference was not the most important one. The really important one came in the introduction where it declared: 'With deep thankfulness to God for the spirit of unity, which by His gracious blessing upon us has guided and controlled all our discussions on this subject, we agree on the following statement and recognize that there is in connection with this subject no ground for maintaining division between the Churches' (*Doc. Hist.*, p. 40).

One naturally tends to be a little suspicious of the exuberance of such language. But even when that is discounted, what remains is still exciting enough: what once divided us on this point, no longer divides us today, of that we are convinced. So far as the doctrine of grace is concerned, the scandal of church division need not continue. To work at the materials of a thousand years of conflict over and over again until point after point is ticked off as no longer a ground for division — that is what Faith and Order has been all about.

There have been a number of such breakthroughs and there is no need to set them all down here. It is already clear what the question was which had to be asked at Louvain. But at least two points still call for explicit mention. Occasionally in the course of Faith and Order's work, traditional sources of conflict have literally vanished into thin air, simply because of a change in the scientific theological assessment of a problem and in the approach to it. This was apparent in the preparations for the Fourth World Conference on Faith and Order in Montreal and at the conference itself where the subject of 'Scripture and Tradition — Scripture or Tradition' was on the agenda. This theme had been hotly debated for centuries. Biblical scholarship had come to the conclusion that the Bible documents the development of a tradition over many centuries. In this process the traditional faith had itself been handed on from generation to generation. It had constantly needed reinterpretation in new historical situations. Even the New Testament itself was simply one stage in this process. And the handing on process continued and continues in the Church. There is therefore a constantly moving interaction going on between the canonical tradition and the post-biblical tradition. Qualitatively, it is no longer possible to draw a hard and fast line between them. The canonical history of the promise and of faith *is* the history of a tradition, and the history of the tradition of faith is an ongoing succession of reinterpretations of the tradition in the light of new historical experience and challenge. This being so, however, the alternative 'Scripture *or* Tradition' simply melts away. It no longer makes sense in those terms. Scripture *is* Tradition and Tradition *is* the way the Church lives with and handles Scripture. And there is no other way.

It should be noted that the disappearance of the old way of putting the problem does not mean the disappearance of the problem itself which underlies the controversy between the churches. It simply shifts its ground and reappears in the question as to the hermeneutical keys used by the Churches to unlock the Scriptures. But no church can now defy the others with an unyielding '*Sola Scriptura*'. This battle-cry no longer has any clear meaning. Nor, on the other hand, can any church now evade the question of the legitimacy and consistency of its own traditional history and interpretation simply by using the old counter-slogan 'Scripture *and* Tradition'. Above all, the churches are all of them confronted inescapably with the fact that the process of tradition and interpretation continues today. It is no more possible to appeal to a closed tradition than it is to appeal to a Scripture insulated from its historical context. So the problem is a contemporary one. All the parties to the dispute have the task of interpreting and handing on the faith *today*, continuously with their own history and in the light of the contemporary situation. And this they can basically only do together, or at least in dialogue with each other.

Even more momentous was the growing realization since Edinburgh 1937 (cf. *Doc. Hist.*, p. 42 ff.) that there were other factors involved in the process of church division (and therefore in that of church reunion, too) besides the religious and theological ones which only theologians could understand. To the serious student of church history, of course, this had always seemed self-evident. Nor was it anything really new to the colleagues in Faith and Order. They knew that the problem of unity in the ancient Church had always been a political problem, too; a problem of the Roman Empire. They knew how much the course of the

Reformation had been influenced by political, economic and social factors. What they did not know, or had not sufficiently taken into account, was the extent to which an almost inextricable tangle of both 'theological' and 'non-theological' factors[18] had influenced and continued to influence the very materials with which Faith and Order itself was specially concerned, namely, the doctrines and structures of the churches themselves. It was not simply that the political and cultural environment helped to determine the policy of the churches in the broadest sense. We always knew that. But it had deeply ingrained itself, incarnated itself, *in* the documents and *in* the structures, in the religious styles, motives and attitudes. The somewhat unfortunate term 'non-theological factors' was quickly dropped, therefore. For these general social and cultural factors, having left their imprint on the development of doctrine and order as such, were therefore theologically relevant, and the formulæ of theology had always had cultural and social coefficients.

In the work of Faith and Order, from Edinburgh (1937) onwards, through Lund (1952) and Montreal (1963), and later, this problem was given more and more attention. It became increasingly clear that working at church unity was not just a matter of the theological study of specifically theological material. It also called for critical inter-disciplinary work in a total context of which the question of Church and Society was an integral part. From 1955 onwards (Study on Institutionalism), interdisciplinary problems and studies played an ever growing part, with limited and sometimes no success (cf. Study on 'Spirit, Order and Organization'). Finally, in Louvain itself — and the conference was important not least on this score — an interdisciplinary subject was taken as the *main theme*, with the relevant methodological problems receiving full attention and not treated as of subsidiary importance. Indeed, these problems were tacitly regarded as a major theme in the form of the question: How do we do theology when the enormous complexity of the problems of church division and church unity stares us in the face?

The risk of calling things by their right names was fully accepted for the first time. Previously we had thought it sufficient to use so-called 'auxiliaries' in theological work;

now we asked quite openly how we could ever in future
possibly dispense with the approaches of social psychology,
social science, and even the materialist critique of ideology
(*Minutes*, p. 62 f.).

Meanwhile, consideration had already been given to the
implications of this new direction of thought. It was first of all
essential to bring out into the open the aims and the strategy
of Faith and Order and at least to show that the
Commission's work had been neither useless nor esoteric. We
have now to ask what the 'negative consensus' — the
consensus about what 'no longer divides' — looked like at
Louvain against that background.

And the probability is that, once we are able to see Louvain
in proper perspective, it will be remembered primarily, not for
the discussion of the main theme 'Unity of the Church —
Unity of Mankind' (what was interesting about that
discussion was not its results but the reasons why they failed
to materialize), but for showing almost incidentally,
particularly in the sections and in the studies they discussed,
just how extensive that 'negative consensus' already is,
covering indeed almost the entire range of traditional Faith
and Order themes: the sources and norms of faith, the means
of salvation, word and sacraments, and even, to some extent,
the ministry and ecclesiology, and certainly, too, the
ecumenical goal and how to achieve it.

I repeat, none of these problems has been solved. They will
only be solved when the *churches* can give a *common official*
answer to them and be sure that in saying the same things
together they really' *mean* the same things, or at least
compatible things. But if that proved possible and were
actually to happen, it would be the conciliar act heralding the
general reunion of Christendom! We have undoubtedly still a
long way to go before that point is reached; indeed, for a
whole host of reasons, we have a good deal further to go than
we once thought.

As we have already seen, the Faith and Order consensus is
a much more modest affair. Theologians, appointed by their
churches, certainly agree together that some things no longer
divide, no longer need divide, the churches. They point out
what seems henceforth compatible, in the light of the plurality
of interpretations and forms which is already tacitly accepted

as possible and even legitimate for them as churches which
are members of the ecumenical movement and cooperate in its
work. And set alongside the traditional catalogue of disputed
theological issues, the extent of this compatibility is
considerable. Even in such thorny questions as ministry and
ecclesiology, for example, it is possible today at least to show
how compatibility could be achieved.

3. The Sources

As we have seen, the old controversy 'Scripture or
Tradition' was, so to speak, exploded because of new common
insights in critical theology. But this was only a by-product of
the momentous decision taken at the Third World Conference
in Lund in 1952. Until then the method of 'comparative
ecclesiology' had been used. The churches showed each other
their treasures, compared them and tried to see how far these
treasures were compatible and at what points they cancelled
each other out or changed each other's values.

At Lund a new method was formulated: 'We have seen
clearly that we can make no real advance toward unity if we
only compare our several conceptions of the nature of the
Church and the traditions in which they are embodied. But
once again it has been proved true that as we seek to draw
closer to Christ we come closer to one another. We need,
therefore, to penetrate behind our divisions to a deeper and
richer understanding of the mystery of the God-given union of
Christ with His Church. We need increasingly to realize that
the separate histories of our churches find their full meaning
only if seen in the perspective of God's dealings with His *whole*
people' (*Doc. Hist.*, p. 85 f.).

Clothed in the esoteric language of texts of the ecumenical
consensus, this amounted to a decision to return to the
sources: *ad fontes*! It was not sufficient simply to confront and
compare what the churches had become in the history of their
division. They needed to return — together! — to the original
source of the Church, to the event of Christ which gave it
birth. They had to discover — together! — why that event
produced the Church and in what way. For there, at the
original source of the Church, only there, was the source of its
unity also to be found.

KANSAS SCHOOL OF RELIGION
UNIVERSITY OF KANSAS
1300 OREAD AVENUE
LAWRENCE, KANSAS 66044

This was a momentous decision in every respect. To return to the original source together meant being ready to receive its criticisms individually and in the others' presence. It meant submitting oneself as well as others, and in their presence, to a process of radical qualification, and this at the one place where such radical qualification is inevitable — namely, the event of Christ as attested by his first witnesses.

Methodologically, this meant advancing from comparative to critical ecclesiology: ecclesiology seen in the critical light of christology.

A common study of the source was therefore necessary. And, in the Faith and Order context at least, this produced a veritable ecumenical landslide. Sharply expressed, the sources lost their normative character. It turned out that what had been normative had not been the source itself but the particular *use* of the sources which had been canonized in each particular tradition *in the interests* of that tradition.

The Bible is not a book but a library. It is not a closed collection of Christian axioms but many voices in open struggle for the truth. And the history of the ancient Church is the continuation of this struggle. Among those engaged in the struggle, there is a consensus — the event of Christ to which they all appeal, and the Christian experience which binds them together — but this consensus is only realized *in* controversy among the biblical and ancient church witnesses. And this controversy is not something dragged in arbitrarily and artificially. It is inescapable because salvation can only be proclaimed as it is at the same time interpreted. And the whole rich range of interpretations has been determined, in part, by the situations to which these interpretations are addressed. It is impossible to siphon off the consensus. It is not a definitive consensus but an open, always contemporary, consensus, produced in particular conflicts and with conscious reference to these conflicts. And even the way this living consensus is worked out, lived with and used, is essentially pluralistic, contingent and conflict-laden.

Read in this ecumenical way, the sources are inexhaustibly inspirational. But they are not normative in the sense that the controversies of the churches over matters of faith and order could be terminated by reference to them. All traditions appeal to these sources and all are 'relatively' right in doing so. On the other hand, no tradition contains the whole equivalent richness of the biblical witnesses in such completeness as to be able to sidestep the critical question of its unqualified apostolicity. The churches are the heirs of the controversy conducted in the sources of their faith. They cannot achieve consensus — not even consensus about their use and understanding of these sources — by lexicography. From the very beginning, consensus has only been attainable by common consultation and common action in face of contemporary challenges and with a contemporary devotion to the inspirational power of the sources.

It is no adequate explanation of this changed attitude to the sources of the Church's faith to say that it is the result of the general acceptance of historical and critical methods of Bible study and critical theology. It is also true that only in the ecumenical context has this critical method acquired its full, persuasive force. For in this context, it cannot any longer be pressed into the service of a previous hermeneutic decision bearing the hallmark of a particular church tradition. Now it examines, not just in theory but in ecumenical realities, the widely divergent hermeneutic approaches and traditional contexts. It clarifies them, makes them intelligible, *and* relative to each other.

The special significance of the study on 'The Authority of the Bible' (*Louvain*, p. 9 ff.) discussed by the Commission in Louvain probably lies in the fact that, by providing an even clearer statement of this long observed revaluation of the sources, it reminded the churches that the real test of the strength of their common basis in the apostolic tradition was the problem of *contemporary interpretation*. 'If the process of contemporary interpretation is seen as the prolongation of the interpretative process which is recognizable in the Bible, then considerable importance must be attached to the situation at any given time in our interpretation of the Scriptures. Just as the biblical writers responded to a particular situation, so contemporary interpretation is also determined by our own situation. The questions which are put to the text play a large part in the interpretation. Of course the text has its own weight. It poses its own questions, and certain questions which spring from our own situation will find no echo in the Bible. The scope is limited in principle by the reality attested

in it. But the situation with its given elements and open
problems determines the perspective within which the biblical
witness must be read and interpreted. The reports of the
regional study groups make it quite clear that such
situation-conditioned hermeneutic perspectives are inescapable. They should not be branded as bias but understood rather as a method of relating to contemporary
situations. The American group, for example, decided on the
basis of its situation that its hermeneutic perspective was God
the Liberator and that it was from this standpoint that the
biblical witness had to be read and interpreted. The report on
'The Significance of the Hermeneutical Problem for the
Ecumenical Movement' (which had been prepared for and
examined by an earlier Commission Meeting in Bristol in
1967 and provided the context of the immediate pre-history of
the study on 'The Authority of the Bible') had already
pointed out this interplay between questions posed by the text
and questions put to the text (see *New Directions in Faith and
Order*, Faith and Order Paper No. 50, p. 37). *The Bible can only
demonstrate its authority when this interplay is accepted*' (my italics;
Louvain, p. 18).

Here as usual, the Faith and Order Commission was
looking ahead, and, indeed, to the immediate future. The
study document concluded with a section on 'The Use of the
Bible, (*Louvain*, p. 21 ff.) in which the ecumenical movement is
described as the right setting for the contemporary exegesis of
the Bible. The Committee of the Commission which dealt
with the document sharpened this still further by referring to
the aim of a common ecumenical confession. 'The Committee
is convinced that a further study of the question concerning
the unity in diversity of interpretations *within* the New
Testament would be very helpful for the interpretation
demanded of us today. Such a study could also furnish better
premises *for the drafting of statements of common faith in our time*'
(*Louvain*, p. 214, author's italics in last sentence).

Much the same applies to what, at first glance, might
appear to be the strangest of the documents presented to the
Commission in Louvain, the report on the Council of
Chalcedon and its significance for the ecumenical movement
(*Louvain*, p. 23 ff.). But this document was only on the surface
preoccupied with a problem of ancient church history, of

concern only to scholars. For one thing, Chalcedon was of course the source of the division among Christians in the Eastern part of the Roman Empire. Negotiations between the 'Chalcedonian' and the 'Non-Chalcedonian' Orthodox Churches meant, therefore, attempting to resolve the conflict by 'staging' it, i.e. taking up once again the question of the Council of Chalcedon. But the relevance of this theme was far greater even than that.

This study undertakes to do for the Councils, i.e. for the Tradition of the Ancient Church, what hermeneutic biblical studies do for the Bible. It defreezes the dialogue between the churches of the ecumenical movement and sets it in motion once more. A council is not something self-contained. It inaugurates a process of reception, of renewed acceptance (re-reception), and therefore of fresh interpretation in the setting of new conflicts. From this standpoint, the ecumenical movement is itself a process of renewed acceptance of the consensus of the ancient Church.

But above all, this study of the Council of Chalcedon tested the model for the reunion of Christendom which had been on the ecumenical agenda since Uppsala — the model of conciliar fellowship. 'The ecumenical movement helps to enlarge this experience of universality, and its regional councils and its World Council may be regarded as a transitional opportunity for eventually actualizing a truly universal, ecumenical, conciliar form of common life and witness. The members of the World Council of Churches, committed to each other, should work for the time when a genuinely universal council may once more speak for all Christians, and lead the way into the future' (*Uppsala Report*, p. 17).

Since Bristol 1967, therefore, Faith and Order has increasingly directed its attention to the councils of the Ancient Church. These have proved to be textbook examples of the open consensus which has to be achieved *ad hoc* in each situation, on which the unity of the Ancient Church rested. The oldest model of unity could easily turn out to be also the most up-to-date one, indeed the only viable one since it is the only one which guarantees the possibility of unity in plurality and plurality in unity and in this way matches the distinctive character of Christ's promise.

4. Sacramental Practice

'Concerning agreements already registered by previous ecumenical gatherings: We ask the churches to take careful note of the statement of consensus on baptism . . . and that on the eucharist; to make a response to these statements, if they have not already done so; and to consider using them in their teaching and applying them in practice. . . . We should welcome the publication of the Report on "The Ordained Ministry" together with the comments of our Committee' (*Louvain*, p. 220 f.).

It is easy to miss the explosiveness of this statement of the Committee in Louvain which had the job of examining the studies on baptism, eucharist and ministry. Yet it was in fact an act of protest — clothed, of course, in the restrained style of Faith and Order statements — and an unmistakable attempt to bring pressure to bear on the churches, or at any rate to make them see clearly the pressure under which they had long been placed.

Structurally, Faith and Order has no way at all of 'summoning' the churches. In fact, it has no direct lines of communication with the member churches, still less one which would be 'official' enough to oblige them to respond. Only the Assembly of the WCC, and the Central Committee as its executive instrument, have the right to summon the member churches.[19] But even a 'summons' issued by these official bodies has only moral force and is not binding on the churches. The World Council of Churches is organized powerlessness. The only significance attached to the work of Faith and Order is its theological weight and the commitment of the Commission members who, depending on their position in their respective churches, can and do, of course, to a large extent, try to stir the churches to action. Faith and Order can, within the narrow limits of its financial resources, publish its documents. But no one can insist on them being read (nor are they often particularly inviting since consensus texts do not make very exciting reading).

The fact that the Commission used such relatively strong words of 'exhortation' itself shows that the matter was urgent and deserved the closest attention. And the two statements referred to — 'Ecumenical Agreement on Baptism' and 'The

Eucharist in Ecumenical Thought' (*Louvain*, p. 49 f. and p. 71 ff.) — are important enough.

[Since this chapter was written, matters have been taken a little further, but the author's basic points have lost none of their validity. After Louvain, the texts were sent to the churches. In the light of the responses received, they were revised together with a document on the mutual recognition of ministries. The three texts were thoroughly discussed at the subsequent Commission Meeting in Accra in 1974 and later published under the title: 'One Baptism, One Eucharist, and a Mutually Recognized Ministry' (Faith and Order Paper No. 73, Geneva 1975). The Fifth Assembly of the World Council of Churches in Nairobi in 1975 asked all member churches to send in their comments by December 31st 1976. The replies of the churches were considered at a special consultation in the week following Pentecost in 1977. The Louvain texts have thus initiated a modest process of reception by the churches. *Ed.*]

The two statements referred to registered agreement among the churches in their understanding of their sacramental practice. Measured by the negative criterion of Faith and Order, this agreement really removes any justification for maintaining division in the areas covered. The areas of sacraments and ministry, moreover, were the ones which the First Assembly of the WCC — not least, under the influence of Karl Barth — had singled out as the areas of 'our deepest difference' — a fundamental incompatibility, affecting the whole area of faith and order, in the way 'catholic' type churches and 'protestant' type churches understood and experienced their existence as churches (*Doc. Hist.*, p. 76 ff.). The Lund decision to replace the method of comparative ecclesiology with that of critical ecclesiology had been the response to this gloomy insight of Amsterdam.

The two documents were therefore memos to the churches asking them to take themselves seriously. At the same time, they were a gentle reminder — whether intentional or not — of the distressing fact that the gap between the verbal consensus and the churches' actual behaviour was widening still further. They warned the churches of the urgent need to achieve a clearer understanding of their obligations to *their* ecumenical movement. What moved the ecumenical

movement? In what way did it move the member churches?
How did the member churches themselves move within it?
Surely the game with possibilities had long ago ceased to be a
game and had become a serious business! Surely now it must
at last be taken seriously? Could they really now pretend that
the movement's awareness of the problem *and* of the consensus
did not exist? And if they could not so pretend — and it
seemed obviously impossible — how much longer could they
remain in this state of suspended animation? And if a
'genuinely universal council' did not yet seem possible, surely
some binding interim steps could be agreed on and some
gradual progress be made in that direction? These were some
at least of the questions in the air at Louvain. The
declarations and, above all, the process of their compilation,
at any rate implied a strong sense that such a step beyond the
strategy of the negative consensus was urgently needed.

Not that the Commission wanted to force any precipitate
short-cuts on the churches. The documents mentioned were
simply appendices to the study reports and lent no colour to
the idea that the 'business of the sacraments' was settled.
Indeed, in the case of baptism, it was rather the opposite
procedure that was chosen at Louvain (*Louvain*, p. 35 ff.). For
there is a tendency for the churches to lull themselves to sleep
on the mistaken assumption that they already have the 'one
baptism'. What they in fact have is a common *understanding* of
baptism, or at least compatible views of baptism. But they do
not have a common baptismal *practice*, nor do they in practice
automatically recognize each other's baptisms. For one thing,
there are churches — the Baptists, for example, — who still
recognize only 'believer's baptism', i.e. adult baptism, and
who re-baptize converts from churches which practice chiefly
infant baptism. For another thing, in the Roman Catholic
Church, for example, we find the custom of rebaptizing
converts on the ground that the ceremony in the churches from
which these converts come had not been properly performed
— a custom which is difficult to understand and almost
impossible to eradicate. Again, there are church communities
— the Kimbanguists, for example — which do not practice
baptism at all, even though they completely agree with the
other churches in affirming what the sacramental sign
denotes. Fourthly, there is the problem of the indiscriminate

baptism of infants in the traditional established and national churches, even though the people who ask for it understand it simply as a social rite of passage. Are these baptisms acceptable in an ecumenical sense? Finally, in many confessions there is a growing body of criticism directed against sacramental signs as such. Do these signs still have any relevance whatever for post-Enlightenment man? Do they not serve rather to obscure the very thing they are supposed to make visible and intelligible, which they indeed did make visible and intelligible in earlier times which were still familiar with magic practices and an essentially effective range of symbols?

Taken as a whole, therefore, the consensus on the theology of baptism is more apparent than real. This is just what the study on 'Baptism, Confirmation and Eucharist' highlights, in a positive and very skilful way. Aided by the theory of the unity of Christian initiation discovered in the practice of the Ancient Church, it shows that agreement on the theology of baptism had proved relatively easy only because baptism had been isolated from its contexts. Water baptism, anointing or the imposition of hands as symbolizing the gift of the Holy Spirit, and first communion, together constituted integral parts of *one* liturgical event in the early Church. Taken together, they represented the separation of the Christian from his previous life-context and his incorporation into the 'Body of Christ' which now constitutes his new and just as all-inclusive life-context. They symbolized a dramatic and at the same time comprehensive transformation of the relational field in which a person lived: a new life (baptism as symbol of participation in Christ's death and resurrection), a new spirit (symbolized in confirmation), a new community in and through which the person henceforward lives (the eucharistic community), in whose corporate identity, strength and destiny he participates from now on just as completely and inclusively as and even more so than he did in the collectives from which he comes. In the Ancient Church, all this in its entirety — especially since it comes as climax to a long and strenuous period of preparation (catechumenate) — had an extraordinarily eloquent significance, indicative of the complete transformation of life's conditions and relationships. It still had significance in the all-embracing symbiosis of

church and society which characterized (and deceived) the
West, although an altered significance. The collective into
which the individual was in this way initiated — now in a
series of disconnected acts — continued as before to be all-
inclusive and total. Only outside the associations were the
sacraments gradually individualized and spiritualized until
the symbolism no longer corresponded with the meaning they
were intended to convey to the believer's soul.

The exciting thing, of course, is the possibility that the
symbols which had become dumb may be beginning to speak
once again in the ecumenical context. (In churches of the
'catholic' type, of course, which had continued always to see
themselves more and more as a messianic collective, they had
never become as 'dumb' as they had in Protestantism.) In a
new way, of course! For in the light of the ecumenical utopia,
the difference between the 'old' (parochial) and the 'new'
(universal) life-context is a dramatic one and therefore one
which can be dramatized in symbols.

In ecumenical sacramental theology, therefore, we are
witnessing an unmistakable 'readaptation' of the sacraments.
Not an illegitimate one, for all these possibilities of a new
understanding are strongly supported in the biblical tradition
and that of the Ancient Church. Within the spectrum of
traditional interpretations, however, priorities are evidently
being revised.

Firstly, there is a new stress on the *social* significance of the
sacraments. The individual is coming to be seen, and to see
himself, in a new life-context, at once all-embracing and
collective. Being universal, this new life-context is in critical
opposition to all the local limitations and parochial divisions
characteristic of human life in its 'natural' communities. At
the same time, however, it is also intensely local in a new
sense. This universal de-restriction is itself localized, made
concrete and livable, in the local eucharistic community.
Here, in the local community, there is henceforward 'neither
Jew nor Greek, neither slave nor free, neither male nor
female'. Here, in the local community, is one encampment of
the one universal messianic people on its journey through
history.

Secondly, the *eschatological* significance of the sacraments is
also coming to the forefront. The ecumenical utopia is, of

course, a concrete one, capable of anticipation in concrete forms and of becoming, via these anticipations, a reality, piecemeal. Yet even as a concrete utopia it never ceases to be eschatologically qualified. That de-restriction — man's full and completed reality made real in the indestructible communion of brothers and sisters, unafraid because no longer under sentence of death — can be concretely anticipated in the local community. Yet each anticipation is once again a restriction. In turn it again erects barriers. It excludes as well as includes. It not only establishes life, it also costs lives. It not only offers integrity but also the possibility of losing it. While it certainly endows those who share it with greater freedom for one another, it also, like all concrete life, once more restricts freedom by a structure which must serve the interests of the larger whole. Every concrete anticipation of the fullness of salvation is also accompanied by a loss of fullness. The sacraments are, therefore, at one and the same time, vehicles *and* custodians of the superabundance of the promise. They not only make salvation concrete but also hold its surplus value open over against all concrete anticipations.

Thirdly, there is a new stress on the *ethical* significance of the sacraments. In their unity — in the non-repeatability of baptism, in the repeated renewal of the covenant in the eucharist, and in the constancy of the presence of the Spirit and with Him the learning process His presence guarantees, symbolized in confirmation — the sacraments signify the obligation of a new life-style and acceptance of this obligation of a new and constantly renewed practical way of life. 'Life created by baptism can best be described as living in communion with Christ in anticipation of the coming of God's kingdom' (*Louvain*, p. 43). But this means a mobile religious life. Anticipating the 'kingdom' a continuing attack on all denials of the 'kingdom', and these denials are constantly being renewed both within and outside the Christian community. The sacraments point to the possibility and to the responsibility of repeatedly transcending whatever undermines hope, cripples love and impugns faith; to the possibility and to the responsibility of again and again liberating life from the social and biographical pressures in which it is trapped; in short, to the possibility and responsibility of struggling against sin, which in this context means literally everything which obstructs the movement and growth of human beings towards their eschatological destiny, everything by which they themselves obstruct this movement and growth.

Finally, there is a new stress on the *missionary* significance of the sacraments. The sacraments insert and keep us in a community which points not merely to the one universal Christendom but also to the one universal humanity. For in the Bible the kingdom of God is promised not just to the Church but to the whole of humanity. All the ecumenical emphases just mentioned in connection with the sacraments point beyond themselves. The solidarity into which we have been taken is the solidarity of all humanity. The eschaton reserved for us is that of the whole cosmos. The new life we are called to live is a life of existence on behalf of all mankind. What distinguishes the Church from the total life of humanity, as the Church understands it, is simply its acceptance of the calling of the whole human race to eschatological salvation. The Church itself *is* humanity already on the way to this goal, the goal of all mankind. And its task is to draw all men into the movement towards this goal. To this extent, the sacraments are signs of a relationship which transcends the church-world divide. Faith and Order ventured, in the form of a question and, for the moment, only in quite exceptional instances, to envisage a eucharist which also transcends the boundaries between church and non-church. 'In missionary obedience in the world all Christians are prepared to cooperate with Christians from other churches. Yet how can we restrict the fellowship of worship to a circle narrower than that appropriate for mission? That question frequently arises among Christians, all of whom have been baptized. But at the same time the problem of the Church's borderlines is being raised in an even wider sense. For in missionary obedience Christians will frequently be sharing a common purpose with men of other traditions of religious faith or who believe themselves of none. How can their occasional demand to be admitted to the eucharistic fellowship of the believers be met in a pastoral way so that they are drawn into the fellowship with Christ instead of being estranged from it? Though the eucharist is clearly the worshipping act of the Christian community, the questions they may raise about their presence and participation need to be faced' (*Louvain*, p. 62 f.).

The two documents, 'Baptism, Confirmation and Eucharist' and 'Beyond Intercommunion', are closely interrelated. Both deal with the coherence of the Church's sacramental practice. What was said earlier, therefore, with particular reference to the document on baptism, applies also *mutatis mutandis* to the document on the eucharist. Both deal with 'refocussed' liturgical actions, closely interconnected. At the heart of both documents we find statements affirming a change in the Church's self-understanding which comes to concrete expression in changes in sacramental theory and praxis. Both documents deal directly with sacramental practice, including questions as to the form of liturgical celebration in each case, proposals for liturgical reform in the widest sense. Each provides an appendix containing a summary of a consensus already formulated but not yet implemented among the member churches.

In the document on the eucharist there is, in addition, a special emphasis. For, both historically and materially, the Lord's Supper is the rite in which Christians and churches receive, celebrate, set forth and consummate their unity in faith. To be divided at the Lord's Table, therefore, means being divided completely, holding each other excommunicate. To come together again at the Lord's Table means consummating and celebrating union. For the member churches of the World Council, to celebrate the eucharist together would be the act of reunion of Christendom itself, whatever other legal steps would still need to be taken. Eucharistic fellowship *is* church unity.

This is why the problem of eucharistic fellowship is the most stubborn of all questions, indeed *the* problem of the ecumenical movement. Once this problem is solved, the goal will have been reached. Those churches which have most carefully preserved the centrality of the eucharistic celebration (Orthodoxy, the Roman Catholic Church, the Anglican Communion) are therefore the ones who are most watchful lest any action be taken under the impulse of triumphalist impatience, and union be demanded when there is still no basis for it. For them, only complete unity can be celebrated eucharistically. But the other churches, not so

firmly tied by such a developed eucharistic tradition, and
therefore more easily inclined to go along with this
'readaptation' of the sacraments, maintain that the Lord's
Supper can itself be a way, an instrument, an effective
anticipation of this unity, even and especially in its
eschatological dimension. We can, indeed we must, also
celebrate the unity for which we hope and for which we work.
We can, indeed we must, celebrate the certainty of the goal
and in doing so draw nearer to that goal.

But this divergence of views, which is becoming
increasingly real and painful not only at ecumenical meetings
and in common action at the world level but even at the local
level, in the specific question as to the possibility of
'intercommunion', makes it increasingly difficult for both
parties to the conflict. The 'catholic' churches cannot close
their eyes to the fact that the ecumenical fellowship of the
churches has developed much further than finds expression in
ecumenical definitions or in the behaviour of the individual
local churches. They are coming under increasing pressure
from their members, especially from the ecumenically active
youth groups who no longer understand the hesitations of
church leaders in the matter of the eucharist.

The 'protestant' churches, on the other hand, for whom
intercommunion presents fewer difficulties, are only slowly
waking up to the fact that the path being trodden by the
'catholic' churches towards the ecumenical future is a far
more complex one than their own and that the reason for this
is that ecumenism is itself a peculiarly 'protestant' invention
and that 'protestant' priorities have largely determined its
planning and development. They realize that they are playing
with fire when they put too much pressure on the 'catholic'
churches. They might run the risk of splitting the ecumenical
movement or, worse still, of destroying its essential credibility.
It would benefit nobody if the eucmenical utipia were
to be over-hastily constructed according to 'protestant'
specifications and unmasked in this way as a mirage of
spurious goals.

The document considered these two problems; 'The
distinction has often been drawn between those churches
which see the eucharist as the sign of the unity once given and
those who see it as a means of restoring that unity. Now it is

increasingly known to be both; rather than holding out for their particular and polemic standpoint, the faithful Christians are those who try to hold both in balance, taking from each what is true and appropriate for the particular moment on the ecumenical way' (*Louvain*, p. 60). Besides the almost revolutionary statement that the truth is so concrete that what is true here and now may be untrue and inappropriate tomorrow, this recommendation and the praxis it outlines and suggests contains a good deal of tactical wisdom. For what it implies is this: If eucharistic fellowship is the criterion and the expression of the given unity, no longer in dispute, then it is sensible and possible also to give cautious but growing eucharistic expression to the unity actually being lived in the ecumenical movement even though it is impossible to define it. On the other hand, all the churches are, ecumenically, ahead of themselves. What is *in actu* already possible ecumenically, is in general and *de jure* not yet possible between the official churches. What is happening in the churches separately is the development of eucharistic theory and praxis in an ecumenical direction. Eucharistic agreement advances stage by stage to the accompaniment of a clarification of terminology: from 'limited admission' to 'general admission' and from 'mutual admission' to 'common celebration' and even to 'intercelebration', which in practice already amounts to full eucharistic communion. As the rights and wrongs of these stages are examined it is discovered that the inner logic of each presses it forward to the next. This sequence of stages on the eucharistic way does not lay too great a burden on any church community. Each can work at the next step. Each can behave ecumenically without having to make any false compromises. In the humble view of the author, this document on the Lord's Supper is a masterpiece of serious and responsible ecumenical diplomacy.

5.   The Structures

'Divisions in communion have often centred around the question of the ministry. Here, while there is as yet no perfect agreement, there are new and most hopeful approaches towards it' (*Louvain*, p. 61).

The study on 'The Ordained Ministry' (*Louvain*, p. 78 ff.) is therefore directly linked with the studies on the sacraments.

[As already mentioned, the discussion of this report at Louvain led to a second stage in the study on the ordained ministry. A new text was prepared and submitted to the Commission Meeting in Accra in 1974. Together with the statements on baptism and the eucharist it was published and sent to the member churches for their reactions. See 'One Baptism, One Eucharist and a Mutually Recognized Ministry', Faith and Order Paper No. 73. The following pages have been slightly abbreviated and edited in the light of the discussions since Louvain. *Ed.*]

By its very nature, the division of the churches is a eucharistic one. If eucharistic fellowship were possible and were to be universally achieved, this would *de facto* be the reunion of the Church. But the theology of the sacraments is not the only factor which determines this possibility. The really divisive factor is eucharistic practice. And lying at the heart of this practice is the question: 'What makes the sacramental and preaching activity of the Church valid?' What is it that guarantees that salvation is present and imparted in the Lord's Supper as the effective act and renewal of reconciliation? The hard core of division lies in the fact that whereas some churches answer: 'The eucharistic ministry with its quite distinctive hierarchical structure' (though further differences appear in the description of this essential structure), other churches just as emphatically deny the hierarchical structure of the Church's authority to administer the sacraments.

The assertion that there are 'new and most hopeful approaches' towards agreement on this question is therefore anything but incidental. If unity on this point were to prove possible, the penultimate and decisive stage on the way to the reunion of Christendom would have been reached.

It is pretty easy and cheap to criticize the churches for the fact that the core of church division lies in the question of the ministry and that the problem is one of structure. To be sure, structures are a question of power. What is at stake in the ministry is *who* controls the Church. It is a question of religious authority. It is also true that church divisions have always in fact been the result of conflicts about power. These conflicts were never purely religious in character. They have always been, in addition, robust expressions of social and

political interests and church politics, and therefore the
pursuit of power politics by other means, which is only to be
expected considering the role of organized religion in human
society. And, of course, it is only a short step from this to
explain away everything else — the spiritual struggles for true
religion, the convictions as to what is true, the sense of what is
right, the arguments over creeds, doctrine and worship — as
pure rationalization and to reduce everything to the mere
struggle for power, ultimately to the class struggle in the
religious field!

All this is undoubtedly part of the truth, but is it the whole
truth? Even though the analysis of the history of church
divisions in terms of social psychology, sociology, and even of
the materialist critique of ideology, was long overdue and the
exposure of theology as a legitimizing discipline quite
inevitable, such a reductionist picture would still be a gross
oversimplification. Even for Marx — who had only a distorted
version of Christianity to go by — religion was the expression
of real suffering and a protest against it (Caute, *Essential
Writings of Karl Marx*, p. 93). It was both a phenomenon of
alienation *and* an angry protest against it. To use this critical
approach to ideology to belittle Christianity and its history in
this way would be to jettison the plus-value of the promise, the
energy of the protest and the truth by which Christianity lives,
the truth which appeared in Jesus of Nazareth. No doubt the
struggles of Christendom have been profoundly marked by
conflicts between vested social interests, and been subject to
their rules and strategies. But in and through these power
struggles there was also a struggle being waged for that which
makes men free in the struggles of this world and which leads
beyond them, a struggle for that which men must ultimately
set against their alienation, namely, their hope and their faith,
that faith which enables them to persist resolutely in their
resistance.

This ambivalence is also found in the struggle over the
eucharistic ministry. It is not simply the struggle of élitism to
retain its position and its power. The contenders, often
involuntarily, are always involved as well in the struggle for
the best way of preserving and keeping operative that power-
house of human freedom established within history with the
coming of Jesus. Even one who considers himself a militant

Protestant, as I do, cannot deny that the headstrong defence of the independence of the hierarchical structure in the 'catholic' churches, permeated to the core by vested interests as it has always undoubtedly been, was perhaps better adapted in the long run for the strategic defence of freedom, or rather of the power-house of freedom, than the indifference to structures, the spiritualizing of the Church, in certain forms of Protestantism. While the latter may have helped in the short term, in the long run it allowed the Church to become all the more a pliant tool in the social power struggle.

The ecumenical lament about 'our deepest difference' which had been voiced at Amsterdam concerned precisely this decisive point: the appropriate structure of evangelical freedom. 'The essence of our situation is that, from each side of the division, we see the Christian faith and life as a self-consistent whole, but our two conceptions of the whole are inconsistent with each other. . . . The emphasis usually called 'catholic' contains a primary insistence upon the visible continuity of the Church in the apostolic succession of the episcopate. The one usually called 'protestant' primarily emphasizes the initiative of the Word of God and the response of faith, focussed in the doctrine of justification *sola fide*. But the first group also stresses faith, and the second also stresses continuity of the visible Church in some form. . . . Yet even when the conversation is between those who deeply trust and understand each other, there remains a hard core of disagreement between different and total ways of understanding the Church of Christ. Each of these views sees every part of the Church's life in the setting of the whole, so that even where the parts seem to be similar, they are set in a context which, as yet, we find irreconcilable with the whole context of the other' (*Doc. Hist.*, p. 76 f.).

Since it is a radical and total difference which is at stake, the 'new and most hopeful approaches' of which Louvain spoke cannot possibly have been simply a matter of a few details. The change which had taken place, the new flexibility which had been achieved, must have concerned the total view of, the fundamental attitude to the tradition of faith. The rather naïve view of unity which simply adds the different concepts of ministry together by employing the formula: 'all have won and all shall have prizes' would certainly not do. In a tentative sort of way Edinburgh had had something of this kind in mind: 'If the ministry of the united Church should sufficiently include characteristic elements from the episcopal, presbyterian and congregational systems, the present adherents of those systems would have recognized each other's places in the Church of God, all would be able to find a spiritual home in the United Church, and the doctrine of Apostolic Succession would, upon a common basis of faith, attain to the fullness which belongs to it by referring at once to the Word, to the ministry and the sacraments and to the life of the Christian community' (*Doc. Hist.*, p. 60).

Meanwhile, there had been church unions where this had actually worked — in South India, for example. But the cohesive power of this particular model of union lay primarily in the area of mainline Protestantism, within the confines of a single tradition. It succeeded best on the 'mission field' where confessional traditions were already relativized. And, above all, it worked because a tiny Christian minority, working in a climate of newly acquired national independence and faced with resurgent and fully indigenized major religions, could hardly do anything but unite if it wished to survive to continue its mission. It is undoubtedly this sense of missionary urgency which constrains Christians to draw closer together to one another in thought, feeling, action, in the main thrust of their faith, and it is then and in this context that they find it possible to successfully combine their ideas of organization.

And it is probably not least the new situation of Christendom in the emergent world community — the fact that all churches throughout the world are beginning to experience this minority situation, to awaken to their mission and, in the radically and swiftly changing world situation, are finding themselves compelled to revise their priorities, re-examine their ecclesiologies, pool their resources, seize their new opportunities and surrender no longer tenable positions — it is probably this new situation in particular which also is relativizing the old structural conflict, that 'deepest difference', and forcing the churches to think and rethink, and to adopt new strategies.

It is against this background that the ecumenical consensus can be most usefully analyzed, especially in regard to this most difficult point where development also still lags furthest behind. It comes out very directly and clearly also in the document on the 'ordained ministry'.

1. The new *challenges*: The word 'challenge' is one of the magic words of the ecumenical movement. It simply denotes the collapse of the old assumptions about church growth and the specifically ecumenical response to this collapse; namely, the decision not to accept the crisis passively, not to be driven on to the defensive but rather to take a steady look at the changed situation and to see it as an opportunity for renewal and the adoption of new approaches. In other words, not to retreat but to advance. Not that the ecumenical movement is an enterprise for incurable optimists. Advance is simply part of the logic of the ecumenical approach. The ecumenical movement itself *is* the advance of Christendom from a no longer tenable position — that of parochialism — into the wider horizon of the inhabited earth, the inescapable context of the human development of mankind. The founding of the ecumenical movement, the decision to unite in this movement, was itself already a decision in favour of this strategy of advance. Of course we find cases of defensive churchmanship even in the ecumenical movement. But a defensive attitude is hard to sustain in the no-man's-land of transnationalism, in the global forefront of social development. There are no fortresses there to retreat into. That is why reactionary churchmanship is generally combined with anti-ecumenical attitudes and behaviour patterns. In the ecumenical movement, a crisis is, by definition, a challenge; and the right response to a challenge is a forward movement.

In the case of the structures and their core in the concept of ministry, the challenge presents itself concretely in the awareness of a growing marginalization of organized religious life. The latter is becoming more and more peripheral to the social processes which determine the future — technological progress, international policy, global class struggle, changing social structures at all levels, but also, for example, consumption, leisure and education. The Church's life becomes more and more marginal and the traditional ministry largely loses its relevance. This experience is common to all churches, irrespective of their official structures.

Because the ministry was central in the church tradition, its

failure to find a place in the contemporary world has now
become the *Church's* failure to do so, excepting to the extent
that the presence of the Church in the world is recovered via
its members and, ecumenically, through the whole people of
God. But a ministry focussed mainly on the diaspora of
Christians rather than on the assembled congregation calls for
quite different forms, quite different techniques, a quite
different understanding of itself, if for no other reason than
that (as a matter of sheer necessity and long before theology
and canon law had had time to catch up with this
development) the religious role of the laity (the people of God)
as the representatives of the Church and as its agents in
service and mission had *already* been enormously enhanced.

2. The new theological *insights*: Accounts of the ecumenical
movement usually start with this point, contrary to the
principle of ecumenical hermeneutics which recognizes that
the questions put to the sources always to some extent
determine the information received. But there is naturally a
circle here and, because of the way work is distributed in the
World Council, where the analysis of the world situation is
assigned rather to the Church and Society desk or that of
Mission, it can easily seem in Faith and Order, or even
actually be true, that the re-evaluation of the sources sets the
process of re-thinking going. 'Biblical scholarship has come to
the conclusion that it is not possible to ground *one* conception
of church order in the New Testament to the exclusion
of others. It appears that in New Testament times differing
forms co-existed and differing forms developed simul-
taneously in various geographical areas. Furthermore it
is increasingly realized that the forms of ministry in the
apostolic period were historically, socially and culturally
conditioned and that it is, therefore, justifiable or even
necessary in the present time to seek to adapt the patterns of
the ministry to the needs of the current situations' (*Louvain,* p.
84).

[Since Louvain, this aspect has been developed further at
successive conferences and on the basis of comments from
member churches. The relevant paragraphs can be found in
Faith and Order Paper No. 73 on 'The Ministry' §§ 31-33.
Ed.]

The description of the New Testament period in the above

quotation also fits the history of the Ancient Church and the Councils. That history offers no answer to the question of the ministries, even though the monarchical episcopate undoubtedly gained the ascendancy quite early.

But a study of the sources does yield one other very important clue to the question of structure and ministry besides the legitimation of a plurality of contemporary solutions. I mean the attitude to the significance of the 'whole people of God', the priesthood of all believers, in biblical times. Historically and theologically, it just is not true that Christ is communicated to his people through a separate religiously privileged ministry. This was certainly not the case in the structure of any of the New Testament communities. On the contrary, the ministries are 'concretions of grace' (Käsemann), concrete forms of the ministry, the *diakonia*, which always belonged to the whole people. Christ's presence among his people takes theological precedence over his presence in the ministries; the activity of the Spirit in the body of Christ as a whole takes precedence over the Spirit's activity in specific functions within this Body. While there are still differences of emphasis as well as controversies concerning the way different Christian traditions interpret their sources, the fact remains that these still fall within and are subordinate to a basic agreement.

3. *The new praxis:* In their praxis the churches are often far in advance of their theological thinking. A study conducted by the Department for World Mission and Evangelism[20] confirmed something we already knew, namely, that despite the considerable difference in their conceptions of order, the churches choose almost identical solutions when they face concrete 'challenges' in concrete situations. All of them have developed ministries which are no longer purely local but more functional in character. Special training is provided for them. All of them have group ministries where ordained and unordained people share responsibilities side by side. All of them agree on the problems of 'professionalism', i.e. of the traditional ministry — a theologically trained, salaried, life-long official church office. In the tremendous complexity of contemporary life in society, this pattern is no longer an appropriate 'normal' standard for ministry. For churches in the diaspora, and especially in the Third World, it is far too

expensive. In dynamic Christian communities and groups, it easily finds itself at cross purposes with the democratic needs of contemporary Christians since authoritarian and élitist tendencies are built into this pattern of ministry. And, finally, all the churches have always had some experience of charismatic phenomena and this is on the increase today. In the richly varied missionary situation of the churches today, religious leadership is very often the fruit of the free movement of the Spirit rather than of church planning or ordination. In short, all the churches are thoroughly flexible in the practical ordering of their work, are familiar with many varieties of church ministry, and allow many exceptions to the rule in their work.

4. *The new ecumenical experience:* Only in this light can we understand what the ecumenical movement means when it speaks, as it often does, about the importance of the 'existing fellowship'. It does not mean only the experience of ecumenical conferences and official forms of cooperation, which is still confined to very few people. It means that the churches, when they try to produce a tenable theory to explain their new praxis, discover that this praxis is already in fact ecumenical. Whether they like it or not, pastors who work in the universities, in the editorial rooms of the mass media, in the ghettos, in education and health services, in youth work and work with marginal groups, in professional work-groups and in citizens' political pressure groups, are *working* ecumenically. They can no longer confine their attention to Christians of a particular colour. The groups around them are interconfessional, associating Christians and non-Christians in a common endeavour; they may find it necessary to cooperate with other groups which are non-Christian. The church ideal of a clear-cut differentiation between different denominations no longer matches the daily life of the Christian. And although it may be difficult to assess the ecclesiological significance of this 'existing fellowship', which grows all the more intense and imperative as resources diminish in an depressingly obdurate world, it is far too dynamic and much too indispensable for the official church leadership to try seriously to control it by dividing it. Nor do they even wish to do so. For even at their level, they feel the pressure of the 'existing fellowship'; the strength derived from

cooperation and the imperative need to share responsibility for Christianity, for its credibility and influence, in the world. Wherever they may live, whatever their structure, all churches are losing some of their foothold in the social contexts, states, cultures and groups with which they have had traditional ties. And they are discovering that they have a new common basis in a world movement which faces gigantic tasks and has gigantic damages to repair. They no longer have either the time or the energy for the ancient border-fortresses and can less and less be concerned for them with a good conscience.

These four developments in the ecumenical development together constitute a sort of parallelogram of forces which inspires and structures the ecumenical development. The prophets, missionaries and deacons are provoked to action by the 'challenges', the theologians by the sources, the church politicians by the new praxis which they must perforce develop and in some way or other come to terms with, both theoretically and in the ordering of their churches, and Christians by the 'existing fellowship'. But whatever be the point of entry into the ecumenical advance, we have ultimately to wrestle with all these factors and see them as a unity. Then the themes and the strategies increasingly converge in the ecumenical movement. Faith and Order tackles Church and Society themes; ecumenical diakonia and mission relate their theories to the studies of both movements and keep them moving with their questions and demands. Seen in the light of the four conditioning factors we have enumerated, the ecumenical movement long ago ceased to be a declinable option and became quite inescapable.

The Weight of the Ecumenical Consensus

Dear Friend,

I imagine you, having read the previous chapter, saying something like this:

'Faith and Order talk seems to me very much like "speaking in tongues". Not only because it is unintelligible but also because of the passion with which it is insisted that this very unintelligibility is particularly important, has a very particular value, is particularly close to the throne of truth. And it occurs to me that Paul, that star-witness among the theologians, permitted speaking in tongues in public *only* when there were interpreters available.

'For example, I would have liked someone to explain the sacraments to me in words I can understand. I know how important symbols are for human understanding if people are to reach any lasting agreement about the meaning and goal of their common life, about the hope that sustains it and the dangers that threaten it, and to reinforce each other in this way of life. What I don't understand is what makes Christian symbols *more* than symbols, and why Christians constantly insist on magnifying the extra magic which their symbols, just like all other symbols, have undoubtedly always had, and on making acceptance of this magic quality the test of adhesion and fidelity to the tradition.

'I say that quite sincerely. I can quite understand, for example, why Christians refuse to exchange their symbols for supposedly "more modern" ones. I, too, believe that their symbols are almost unmatchable. There *is* no better symbol for the renewal of human solidarity than the common meal. As for the water symbolism, the story of evolution and the

63

findings of psychoanalysis had already taught me far more compelling arguments in favour of its retention than those usually offered by the theologians. But here again, I fail to understand why the churches don't exploit the eloquence of these incomparable symbols more effectively in their celebrations. There seems to me something fishy about the way Christians have reduced "drowning" in baptism to a sort of symbolic morning "lick and a promise", and the banquet celebrating the renewal of the divine covenant to the travesty of a "paupers' meal". I find it a little odd that I of all people should be asking this question but, if Christians treat their symbols in such a cavalier fashion, can they still really believe in what they symbolize? Yes, well. . . .

'So, you see, in my own way, I understand some things quite well, which is precisely why there are other things which I just don't understand at all. Two in particular.'

'Firstly, if the establishment of a consensus really has reached the advanced stage presented in this report, why on earth has it not led to something more than a handful of church unions? Why has it not already culminated in really bold and dramatic acts of reunion? Christians are not usually so dilatory when their own interests are at stake. It seems to me that if they had been able to make their universality, their unity and "catholicity" really visible and effective across all the iron curtains, they would have gained an enormous advantage over all the states, cultures and institutions of this world in its transition to world community.

'I don't think I am cherishing any illusions on this score. I know — and it is noticeable in the texts you cite — that the old conflicts are by no means dead and that new ones cast their shadow over the scene. But if there is anything of interest in this domestic consensus among Christians, it is surely this: that it seems to embody, or at least to make conceivable, something in the nature of a "unity in conflict". Why then do the Christians not play this trump card? The whole of mankind is obviously on the lookout for just such a pattern of unity — since otherwise it cannot survive *and* make radical changes, or make radical changes *and* survive. Admittedly the time may not yet be ripe for the creation of a single international organization of Christians, the "Super Church" excluded at Toronto. Perhaps it may never be needed at all.

But surely there must be provisional solutions? Surely some advance is possible which can be made intelligible to and engage the loyalty of even quite ordinary Christians?'

'Secondly, if, as I assume, this dramatic demonstration of the "family of man" is *not* what the churches want (otherwise the ecumenical movement would surely go much further and much faster!), what on earth has this whole consensus game got to do with the rest of the world? Who does it interest? Who does it benefit? Who does it help? If it is not about this obvious thing, what on earth *is* it about? Contemporary man faces so many serious problems of survival — ranging from the international class struggle to the problem of educating little children so that they do not forever have to shoulder the burden of man's long story of self-inflicted alienation and then as grown-ups to impede and nullify, as if in a trance, every revolution which would benefit them. I know many Christians who are really concerned with these vital questions. With them, real cooperation is possible. But, as it seems, their church organizations consider other things more important, though they could have a real influence in these vital questions, why do they always go on pretending to be the "nub of the world"? Yes, I know, they have their own problems of organizational survival, and they obviously consider them more important than mankind's problems of survival. But in that case, why don't they keep quiet and stop making such a fuss about them? Obviously they can't even beat up enough interest in this ecumenical game the churches are playing among themselves, not even among their own members. What, then, has it got to do with me and my friends?'

I

Of course, I can't be sure I've interpreted you correctly or done justice to your views. However, on examining the ecumenical consensus as documented by Louvain, I find myself left in the end with precisely the same ambivalent impression I have attributed to you. On the one hand, I am still astonished at the measure of success achieved by Faith and Order in the fifty years of its existence by its strategy of 'staging the conflict'. My own personal ecumenical experience was acquired more in Life and Work (or Church and Society, as it is now called); i.e. with the laity and renewal movements, which originally invented the ecumenical movement in the nineteenth century but were then swallowed up and alienated by it as the church institutions took over. With such an apprenticeship, one was inclined to underrate Faith and Order. It was hard to believe that the theologians of all people, experts in division and in producing divisions, could have any great success in creating unity. We were more interested in the dramatic sorties and new departures in the contemporary world, as illustrated, for example, at the Church and Society Conference in Geneva in 1966. We were also easy victims of the optical illusion caused by the fact that it was always much easier to sell ecumenical missions, ecumenical diaconia, ecumenical appraisals of the world situation, ecumenical politics, than it was to sell ecumenical theology. In authentic theological style, Faith and Order always worked and spoke rather *sotto voce,* always emphasizing the difficulties more than the possibilities. At Louvain, I found myself for the very first time right inside the ecumenical workshop. And I discovered that what had been produced in that workshop during the past fifty years could actually be put on display. Far more had been achieved here than anyone had expected, far more than other highly esteemed WCC projects had been able to achieve.

But this only made one want to ask all the more: what weight did this ecumenical consensus *in statu nascendi* really have? Why was it so hard to sell? Why did it make so little difference? And the question at once breaks up into its separate elements.

II

For example, what weight does this work have for the members of the Commission itself? I may be exaggerating, but I found no great enthusiasm in Louvain. Instead I sensed a deep mood of resignation, frustration, confusion and potential aloofness. This had something to do, of course, with the fact that papers and discussions dealing with traditional

Faith and Order problems were by no means the main business at Louvain. The main theme, in fact, was 'Unity of the Church — Unity of Mankind'. In other words, the very question you yourself raised concerning the actual importance of the ecumenical movement for the survival of mankind. And no one could pretend that Louvain was brilliantly successful in its treatment of this question. The next chapter will report on that.

Nevertheless, I do not believe that the apparently sombre mood at Louvain was due to any immediate ephemeral cause. When the chairman of the Commission adopts a dry defensive tone right from the outset in his opening address, when a dyed-in-the-wool ecumenist and staunch Faith and Order enthusiast like Savas Agourides speaks in a low-key about the 'meagre results of fifty years of ecumenical work', when, despite their diversity of themes and styles, almost all the platform utterances strike a basic note of self-depreciation and self-criticism and agree in their criticism of their own causes, when never a single 'wedding garment' is to be seen, never a single festal note to be heard — then however favourably one may be impressed by this complete absence of ecumenical euphoria, of even the most sublimated forms of self-adulation, and of all institutional militancy, one is still left wondering whether, if such an at-best half-hearted commitment had predominated fifty years ago the Faith and Order movement would ever have got off the ground, and who it was, and with what resources, who had actually produced the considerable achievement reflected in the documents. Not even a football team could long survive such a lack of enthusiasm, and even football is child's play compared with the difficult art of overcoming the division of the churches. Not to mention the fact that there's no money in Faith and Order work!

Enquiring further, the next thing to strike us is the peculiar style of the documents. Ecumenical documents in general and Faith and Order documents in particular usually contain more questions than answers or affirmations. The obvious explanation might be that the ecumenical consensus consists, basically, simply of a growing common *awareness* of the problem but it is not yet a consensus as to its *solution*. This is both true and false. A considerable measure of agreement is needed even to be able to formulate common questions. This

is especially the case where the parties in question are not
unskilled in the subtleties of philosophical and theological
debate. Often enough, the formulation of a general *status
quaestionis* means that half the work has already been done.
This is particularly true of ecumenical theology whose first
task is surely to help the churches find their way out of the *cul-
de-sac* of answers which divide them. The high proportion of
questions in ecumenical documents is, moreover, realistic in
view of the fact that *per definitionem* it is only the member
churches, and not the ecumenical bodies, which can produce
common answers in the form of affirmations or official legal
acts. The ecumenical movement is only the 'handmaid' of the
churches (Lausanne 1927). All it can deliver is half-finished
products. It dares not offer more if it does not wish to exceed
its mandate.

All the same, one still has a feeling that, although these
points are valid, they are not the whole truth.

One recalls important points in Meyendorff's address: he
mentioned the 'failure' of Montreal 1963: 'this Fourth World
Conference on Faith and Order had failed in an attempt to
define the ecclesiological nature of the World Council of
Churches, proving implicitly that biblical and traditional
definitions of church unity were still inapplicable to
Christians in their present state of division and that the World
Council of Churches, when it comes to precise statements and
definitions, is still very much bound by the Toronto Statement
of 1950. No understanding of unity can presently be assumed
by all, *and if some formulae can be widely accepted, one can be sure that
they are understood differently in the WCC constitution*' (*Ecumenical
Review*, Jan. 1972, Vol. XXIV, p. 30). This itself takes us a
little further.

The whole consensus which is visible in the Louvain
documents ends, therefore, not with a full stop but with a
question mark which alters the entire character of the
consensus. The question is whether we really mean the same
thing when we use the same words. Unfortunately, this
question cannot be answered with the means at present
available to the ecumenical movement.

Even when someone breaks away from the traditional
question technique and makes in the direction of a
formulation of agreed affirmative statements, as Lukas

Vischer probably had it in mind to do when he proposed that Faith and Order should work on a common 'account of the hope that is in us' (*Louvain*, p. 205 ff.), this question still remains unanswered. It cannot possibly be answered by merely 'playing with the possibilities' of an ecumenical future but only by united action, only by finally embarking on that future and, ultimately, only by that 'genuinely universal council' invoked at Uppsala, only by the reception of such a council by Christians throughout the world, by the local communities who learn of such a council. The only way to find out whether we mean the same thing when we use the same words is together to do what we say. And even when we have advanced to united action, the answer to the question is always *ad hoc*, always moving from one decision to the next. Even in practice, the consensus remains an open one. In any case it will produce fresh conflicts and will then have to be tested again by 'staging' these conflicts. Language never, in fact, produces the degree of unambiguity for which Meyendorff asks. And the only adequate test, the test of practice, is denied to the ecumenical movement. Meyendorff is much too intelligent not to know that.

We suspect, therefore, — pushing the game with words a little further — that Meyendorff meant something different from what he actually said. That he meant to say: Do we actually say *everything* we think when we work on our consensus? Or do we only say that which represents no threat to the 'existing fellowship'? Only what will not prevent the discussion from continuing? And if so, does this not mean that, in addition to what we *say* together, there is also a good deal more that we really *think* but keep to ourselves for the sake of the 'existing fellowship', and the difference between what we say and what we think becomes greater and greater until one day it may become so huge that our theological conscience will be strained to breaking point?

To put it another way. Do we owe the consensus to a peculiar form of 'success syndrome' which makes it impossible for us to reach complete agreement because no one wants to risk complete confrontation, because the object of the discussion is, in fact, carefully to discover the areas of disagreement and equally carefully to avoid them by taking some middle course?

I discussed this question with a Third World friend, a
member of an Eastern Orthodox Church. In a conversation at
the supper table I asked him about the fine dividing line
between ecumenical flexibility and ecumenical dishonesty.
'Alright,' he replied. 'Let me be quite frank. We continue to
consider your churches to be defective. But that is not
something one can possibly go on saying endlessly!'

I swallowed hard for a moment. This is in fact a very tender
spot, even though one would not hesitate for a moment to
admit the defects of one's own church in a spirit of self-
criticism or in discussions within one's own confession. But it
is quite another thing to hear one's own home criticized by an
outsider, to be dismissed as a 'have-not' by people in the
superior position of 'those in possession'. I then tried to
express my own discomfort: 'I am beginning', I said, 'to
understand your eucharistic spirituality, at least in theory,
and even your concept of the episcopal office, at least in
theory. But I miss the reality of the fullness of which you
speak.'

Yet I was aware of how much this left unsaid. It hurts to
hear someone speaking frankly about the flaws of the
Protestant churches. But these flaws are not news to us and
we must know that others think about them, too. After all,
Toronto could not have come completely out of the blue; it
must have had some *Sitz im Leben*. Not even this ultimate
reserve as to whether the other churches are really true
churches robs the consensus of its value. In fact, this reserve
has been taken into account in the consensus, lifted up on to a
higher plane, in true dialectical style. That every single one of
the member churches of the World Council can achieve the
ecumenical ideal of the Church only by development, only by
growth, only by realizing its own buried potential, only by
radical renewal wherever possible and, as it does so, must also
look confidently for growth and renewal at different points in
the other churches, too, this is not really news to any of them,
nor will it really be passed over in silence in the ecumenical
dialogue, even if there must be discretion in the way it is
spoken of. The ambivalence of the ecumenical consensus must
have other causes besides this.

III

We therefore continue with our questions. Was there perhaps some connection between the embarrassment of Louvain at the considerable achievements presented to it and the fact that ecumenical theologians were no longer very clear for whom they are really working or who really takes any serious interest in their work? Put in a different way: What weight does the ecumenical consensus really have for the member churches?

Here we have to recall once more the ambiguity of the mandate given to the ecumenical movement and its agencies. The ecumenical movement is a movement of churches, the formula runs (since 1948). Although that is formally true, it is at the same time quite false. A more accurate description would probably run: the ecumenical movement continues to be what it always has been, a movement of ecumenists (admittedly, since Amsterdam, under the control of the churches).

Nothing that happens in ecumenical commissions is binding on the member churches even if their official delegates have agreed with it. The theory is that the substantial weight of ecumenical work is enough to carry the churches along in its ecumenical wake. And up to now this is what has actually happened, at least to a considerable extent. No one can deny that the world of the churches has been transformed and is now far more ecumenical, far more conscious of its universal horizons.

It is not difficult, of course, to find ways of exercising influence, of controlling or bringing pressure to bear, in both directions. But, taking the situation as a whole, the WCC pays for its freedom of action by its impotence *vis-à-vis* the member churches and the churches pay for their freedom from obligation by foregoing any close control over the Geneva headquarters and its actions. Even at the Assemblies, control is so much in the hands of the ecumenical 'in-group' and of the 'officers' and staff that even large delegations like the German one never feel quite sure that they are not being ridden roughshod over.

That may well have been the best solution for the initial period of the ecumenical movement, sheltering it, as it largely did, from over-anxious reactions in the member churches. But meanwhile it has become increasingly obvious that the ecumenical movement is operating with an overdraft and credit notes of dubious worth. When they move in ecumenical circles, church representatives tend to talk big, to say and promise a great deal. This is not to question their personal sincerity, of course, but in the internal politics of their own churches they often find themselves in no position to redeem their ecumenical promises, or even to interpret them and enlist adequate support for them. An ecumenical maximalism and a denominational minimalism continue unreconciled side by side in the soul of one and the same church leader. The ecumenical bodies and the WCC in Geneva, too, tend to exaggerate the weight of the consensus they are achieving. They build on their documents as if they were building on the massive foundation of a growing ecumenical purpose shared by many millions of Christians throughout the world whereas, in fact, the lines of communication between the ecumenical advance party and the member churches either do not exist or else operate according to communication laws which defy rational control.

A dramatic example of this state of affairs was provided by German reactions to the WCC's Programme to Combat Racism. Unanimity in the ecumenical movement on the issue of racism and its wider implications for world peace and for the credibility of the churches' witness dates back at least to the nineteen-thirties and has become clearer and more militant with every passing year. In a world situation in which institutional racism had become quite intolerable for its now-organized victims, a situation in which the possibilities of verbal protest and token resistance (labelled 'non-violent' in Germany) had been completely exhausted and the churches were at last aware of the power of the powerless which they had themselves deliberately generated, the World Council found itself in a position in which it was obliged to make a move. It had talked so long and so loudly about racism; it was now high time to do something about it. And it even seemed as if it really *could* do something, since on no issue was there such unanimity among the churches.

Then, all of a sudden, just as this — at least symbolically — militant programme was on the point of being implemented in the form of quite small financial grants, the member churches in Germany and even their official leaders appeared to be completely taken aback, indeed, quite unable and unwilling to cope with the problem morally and spiritually. German representatives, responsible people to a man, had from the very beginning been involved in efforts to develop people's consciousness of the problem which had at last moved the Council to act. They had even shared the decision to launch the programme. But there had been no feedback. The large dossier which had been compiled had been available in a German version but was noted only by 'officials' and filed away under 'Ecumenical Movement'. Then, when one solitary provincial church (the Evangelical Church of Hesse and Nassau) decided to endorse the programme officially at its synod (and thus to take the one step that transforms the ecumenical 'game with possibilities' into something serious!), the storm broke.

At the level of the churches, the consensus proved practically non-existent. Church members neither knew of it nor went along with it. There was a public outcry. And some of the local church authorities behaved as if the ecumenical proposal was a subversive act on the part of international communism! No one was being malevolent. There were good and weighty arguments against the Programme to Combat Racism and against the decision of the Hesse Church to donate a hundred thousand German marks. The only trouble was that all this came too late!

What weight does the ecumenical consensus have in the member chrches? It is very difficult to avoid being satirical![21]

IV

The restriction of the ecumenical consensus to ecumenical coteries and its lack of firm roots in the general outlook of ordinary church members has particularly serious effects on Faith and Order. For its concern is with *theological filigree work,* so delicate and intricate that it presents special problems of interpretation. But the real problem is that it is theological work. For what real weight does theology, ecumenical theology especially, carry in the actual praxis of the churches?

Along with theologians in all parts of the world, the Faith
and Order theologians are uncertain as to their precise
function in the churches. Indeed in ecumenical work this
uncertainty is intensified.

Critical theology is generally regarded by the official
churches as a menace. It seems to undermine the religious life
of church members. It treats the sacred sources as historical
documents. It cuts the confessional documents down to size.
It turns out pastors who rebel against the traditional role of
the ministry, who are committed to change in church and
society, who have already in the seminaries gained experience
of permanent opposition to church authorities. It increasingly
introduces into domestic church discussions an experimental
scientific approach to problems and explodes many cherished
illusions. It uses a recondite language and takes little or no
trouble to explain its insights in terms ordinary Christians
could understand. (It isn't just the church authorities who
level this charge — it happens to be the plain truth!)
Theologians have problems about what their role should be.
They refuse to be mere suppliers of ideological systems to
meet the churches' need for self-preservation. That is why
some of them deliberately adopt a critical stance towards the
Church, in a way which church leaders find increasingly
intolerable. Relations between academic theology and the
Church are, to put it mildly, very strained.

In the case of ecumenical theology, relations with the
churches are still more difficult. In all the other burdens
which theology lays on the churches today — the erosive
effects of contemporary biblical scholarship and of the work of
church historians, the systematic theologian's ruthless
probing of the responsibility of Christian talk of God in
the contemporary philosophical climate, the practical
theologian's piling up of empirical challenges to the praxis of
the churches— ecumenical theology now adds the last straw
of ecumenical plurality. In the life of the Church it is not too
difficult to keep scientific claims at arm's length for quite
some time, either by ignoring them or neutralizing them, or
else by pointing out (quite correctly) that there is a greater
obligation to church members than to the changing fashions
of critical theology. What is far more difficult to deal with,
however, is the suggestion that other churches are the Church

in a different way, more fully, more convincingly, more credibly, more successfully, with greater fidelity to their origin, and these churches *are* really there! These other patterns of Christian life and church life are no longer remote. They are quite close and getting closer. Their reality affects us, whether church leaders like it or not. Because of the challenge of ecumenical theology, an exclusive claim to represent the Christian tradition is no longer possible either theoretically or in practice.

But it isn't only in relation to church institutions that ecumenical theology has problems. Still more important for it is the question as to how its work relates to Christian life as actually lived in the congregation. People are more deeply provincial than they realize. They have a deep attachment to, a profound involvement in their native place. And in some ways the claim made by Faith and Order theologians cuts far deeper than the challenge of biblical exegesis, dogmatics or practical theology. For what it is after is not just to make people more contemporary, more up-to-date, in their ways of thinking about the Christian faith but also to reorient their religious life and their consciousness towards the future. It tackles not only the contents of belief, but also deeply rooted attitudes of mind, prejudices, motives and patterns of behaviour. It expects people to learn to look beyond their own borders, to enlarge their sensitivity and their life-style. It expects them to abandon their hostile images. The strange must cease to be strange to them. Change is to be welcomed instead of feared or condemned. God must be transplanted out of the past and become known and welcomed as the One who has always already moved ahead into the future. The Church must cease to be only the familiar past and become instead the longed-for future. All this adds up to an education which is far more radical than any merely intellectual one. In the last analysis, of course, even a theology which is not explicitly ecumenical is also after this deeper learning, but it certainly does not stretch the imagination of faith nearly as much as does theological thinking with a world outlook which has still to be transformed into a moral and spiritual reality.

At the same time, however, ecumenical theologians appear to be professionally infatuated with the particular, the traditional, the local, with all their limitations. Certainly it is their business to reconcile the particular with the universal, the traditional with the concrete historical future, continuity with change. Their concrete utopia envisions a united world-wide fellowship of faith, pregnant of the future, in which a Christianity which is still rooted in stone age magic as in many parts of Africa will be reconciled with the timeless ancient church spirituality of Athos, with the secular religion of Europe 'after the death of God' and with the Latin American faith in the Christ of revolution, with the Pentecostal enthusiasm of the American ghetto and the second religious vitality of the Jesus People, really united and not simply reduced to the level of some ecumenical conformity. No vision could be more imaginative than this and none is more needed today. But how is it to be integrated into the thinking of our own local congregations?

There is, of course, a third group — the impatient ecumenical *avant-garde*. For this group, Faith and Order work is undoubtedly Christian archaeology or, worse still, Christian obscurantism, a massive attempt to turn back the clock of faith. The very fact that we ourselves are half-inclined to go along with this group helps us to realize that if it gained the upper hand it would inevitably disturb the precarious equilibrium of contemporary ecumenism

Who are the ecumenical theologians working for? Who wants their work? Who *really* wants it? On whose behalf do they push forward ecumenically?

V

The analysis must be pressed further. Ecumenical theology, earlier than the provincial theologians, discovered that here were factors at work in the development and division of the churches which also determine what is possible ecumenically, factors which nevertheless cannot be theologically controlled, indeed cannot even be appropriately perceived and examined theologically.

Ecumenical theologians know from their own experience, for example, the divisive effects of language. Like poetry and humour, or the intimate language of lovers, religious experiences and theological modes of thought are especially resistant to translation. Even in the passage to and fro across the frontiers between the three 'official languages' of the ecumenical movement, much remains unsaid and unsayable. But besides French, German and English, there are also Hindi, Swahili, Arabic. . . . What language did the Pentecostal Spirit speak?

Ecumenical theologians know how vulnerable cultural identities are and how inevitably they will go on being wounded, even in the ecumenical dialogue. They understand why black Americans are trying to root the white Christ out of their hearts and to invent a black Christ, by a black theology,[22] a black spirituality, black underground churches. They understand this because all of them who are not Europeans or white Americans are wrestling with the same temptation. All of them have to overcome the same repugnance when they see the blond Nazarene, this gentle accomplice of a far from gentle destruction of the world. But they also know that the ecumenical future is probably unattainable along that road. For the Christ we seek is neither black nor white but, like the Galilean peasant, the colour of the earth and must first of all become a stranger to us all in order to be the neighbour of us all, must be the human man who binds all of us together because he will allow none of us to exploit him as a weapon against his neighbour.

They know the intolerable tension between the strategy of nation-building, the creation of new nations out of the ruins of colonialism, and the ecumenical wisdom of 'international man' who knows no frontiers. They realize that nation-building is not to be evaded but also the price that churches and Christians, and indeed anyone else, have had to pay for identifying themselves too closely with particular goals and values. From their experience of the white world, they know that it is difficult to survive the winding-up of such associations, even if there is no escaping the indigenization process which will inevitably produce such associations.

Ecumenical theologians know all this from bitter experience over many decades. They also know that theology cannot produce anything capable of overcoming the divisive effect of these factors, not even in theory. For the divisive factors are already operating even in theology itself.

They also know, at least in part, how to tackle this problem. They know it would need an interdisciplinary group working on the problem on a long-term basis. They know that, in Faith and Order, theologians have to sit down and listen to ethnologists, cultural anthropologists, linguistic scientists, psychologists and experts in social psychology, and, not least, with sociologists. But they know, too, that the non-theological factor which presents the greatest problems in ecumenical work is the theologian's own incapacity for dialogue. This is partly connected with his style of thinking, partly with his professional idiosyncracies, but also partly with his subject matter. The fact is that theologians have to deal with three quite different sorts of data. Theology is a hermeneutic discipline: it has to explore and understand documents and historical events, and interpret them intelligibly. But it also has to deal with a religious institution, its structures and functions, with a social system which is only accessible to an empirical and multi-dimensional investigation. Thirdly, in these documents and in this social system, it is dealing with an experience which claims the status of revelation. And, in relation to this claim, far from being impartial and uncommitted, theologians have traditionally been charged with affirming its truth within the prevailing philosophical climate of their time and, if need be, in opposition to it. There is no way in which these three different kinds of data can be made commensurable, no way of harmonizing them in water-tight theories or directives for praxis. Whether, in view of this 'impossible' task, theology can still claim to be a 'science', is not the real problem. The real ecumenical problem is that the 'impossibility' of its task makes theology an unsatisfactory partner in the interdisciplinary dialogue. The unsatisfactory outcome of the discussion on 'Unity of the Church — Unity of Mankind' was one illustration among several in Louvain itself of this basic problem of theology.

The Fourth Assembly in Uppsala noted a convergence of all ecumenical studies upon anthropological problems. It made the theological question of the *humanum* a key issue and appointed a coordinator, Canon David Jenkins. Canon Jenkins was present at Louvain. He brought to his task an unusual competence in many disciplines and a rare passion for theology. His interim report at the time of Louvain was that the theological question of the *humanum* was in the last analysis the question of — how to do theology today.[23]

VI

1. Modern developments, of course, do not have to be interpreted as new *challenges,* new opportunities for the churches, for their mission and renewal. It seems more obvious to regard them as processes which drive the Church more and more on to the defensive and make ecumenical renewal less and less likely.

A year before Louvain, Church and Society had organized the first great study conference on the new theme of technology and futurology.[24] This had brought together, in hitherto unprecedented numbers, scientists from all the disciplines which are specially relevant today for the future of mankind. Their analysis of the problems of human survival — environmental destruction, population explosion, genetic disaster, the problems of urbanization and industrialization, the production and growth society with all its cultural presuppositions, the continued extension of electronics to new areas of social life and, with it, the manipulation of human beings on an unprecedented scale — produced a nightmarish picture. This was all the more so if one took seriously the persistent interventions of Third World representatives present, insisting again and again that all this was a disaster which scientific technological civilization had brought upon its own head. They warned us not to overlook the world-wide civil war which that civilization had spread across the globe, the world shortage of food, the impoverishment of the majority and growing disparities in the distribution of resources, of education and political power. 'Don't forget the institutionalized racialism of your technological way of life and your world planning! You are finished and you are dragging us down with you!'

There were other voices, of course, more positive and optimistic. Most of the problems of survival were undoubtedly soluble. But the political institutions which could solve them were lacking. There was no public opinion to insist on their solution. There was no readjusted system of norms and values, no relevant contemporary morality, to point the way to their solution.

The scientific data piled up to show the unpleasant prospects for mankind were depressing enough. But they were not the really alarming aspect of this conference. The really frightening thing was that all the disciplines represented at it, without exception, were asking for guidance, for a convincing proposal for the human development of mankind by which to measure and control technological development and forward planning. They no longer confidently assumed that they themselves could produce such a proposal. That was something quite new. They knew *what* man could do and *how* he could do it but not what he should do it *for*. To answer that question they had neither the method nor the moral courage. Was no one able to say anything, then, to point the way forward in this world of perfect instruments and confused motives?

The theologians at the conference maintained an almost complete silence! They proved to be the biggest disappointment of this scientific gathering. They had practically nothing whatever to say, though this was partly due to the way the consultation was organized. In an almost complete overhaul of his approach in *The Secular City*, Harvey Cox suggested that we should perhaps quite deliberately accept 'irrelevance' and refuse to give the answers to the problems of technology which the world expected from us. 'What we should do at certain points in history is to nurture a kind of quaint, strange and even erratic dimension, sometimes expressed as much through the grotesque or strange as through the relevant and the concrete. That is not, I would hasten to add, the entire mission of the Church. But perhaps many of us in this room who have laboured hard on theology and social ethics have overlooked the fact that at times the Church can be so in step with its times that no one notices it. To be a little out of step with one's time is to call some attention to the way in which the steps are moving.[25]

Could be! But we have to face up to the fact that this is a retrograde step, a withdrawal, resignation in the full sense of the word.

It means relinquishing the deeply felt conviction which has given the relevance of the Gospel of Christ to the contemporary world a central place in the thinking of the ecumenical movement.

It was not the purpose of the Church and Society consultation in Geneva to produce theological answers, of course. The idea was to formulate the problem, not to deliver its solution. But the same air of gloom was noticeable even in Louvain, the same brooding question whether world developments had not long since left the Church behind, not just in the sense that the Church had culpably failed to keep abreast with them but in the much more radical sense that perhaps all the forms of contemporary distress were in the end incommensurate with the promise of faith. And even if one answered this question affirmatively, there was still the other question to be answered: in what language was this commensurability to be communicated? The Catholic theologian Joseph Ratzinger commented: 'When one considers the effects of technical civilization upon the unity of mankind, a remarkable contradiction comes to light. On the one hand, technology has developed into a comprehensive form of life and thought; in the language of technology there is an unbroken possibility of communication across all barriers. On the other hand, and at the same time, with the advance of the kind of positivistic thinking which technology encourages, the language of philosophy has become more and more fragmented, so that philosophy today consists for the most part only of philosophies which exist very largely without communication side by side. Hand in hand with the universalizing of technological communication goes a breakdown in communication in the questions of meaning, in the realm of the really human, which no longer appears to be communicable. The unity of mankind is thus more sharply threatened than ever before in the very midst of the outward process of unification.'

'In this process . . . faith has lost its language, or it now only speaks an esoteric language which is only understood by Christians but almost defies translation into the language of those outside and has even created insuperable problems between certain groups within the individual churches. Is the Church really condemned to be speechless in the technological world, to pluralism in communication, to the ghetto?' (*Minutes,* p. 58).

2. The fresh *theological* insights — the pluralism of the sources of the faith and the historical reasons for it, the realization that the unity of faith and the Church only exist *in* the struggle for truth and in an open *ad hoc* consensus which is itself in turn marked by conflict — undoubtedly gave a new

flexibility to the use of the sources and to ecclesiology in all the churches, made dialogue fruitful, made possible new unions between churches, and convinced churches of their structural freedom and of the possibilities of growing together.

That is only *one* possible interpretation, however. The other is simply the basic experience of Ernst Troeltsch: 'Everything is falling apart!' There is no longer any firm foundation of common faith and religious cooperation whatever, not even within one and the same church, let alone the broader ecumenical scene. We no longer have any criteria by which to distinguish between a legitimate plurality of permissible responses of faith to the Gospel and an unlimited religious pluralism in which all is relative, where all are partly right and partly wrong, and where convincing arguments no longer convince.

This is the lament of the fundamentalists, old style and new, whether naive or deeply reflective. It is not just that they are shy of change. What disturbs them is the question: is there still any basis for religious authority? In other words, how can judgement and pardon, warning and encouragement, guidance and assurance, celebration and anticipation, still have that degree of authority which is vital if the Church is still to remain the Church? Their solution, the break-neck leap into sheer decisionism, is impossible. But their awareness of the problem is one which no Christian may evade. In every Christian, every theologian, every ecumenist, there is a hidden fundamentalist. And this fundamentalism casts its shadow over every consensus formula. How far does the consensus go and what weight does it have for people wrestling with the meaning and meaninglessness of their existence, its truth and untruth, its hope and its menace, its courage and its despair, whose needs are simply sidestepped by guesses and hedgings and carefully balanced alternatives?

The Greek representatives in Louvain came fresh from a dispute in their own church in the course of which some had asserted that the word 'ecumenical' was a synonym for the word 'diabolical'. The devil, *diabolos,* is the one who throws everything into confusion. He is the author of chaos, the sower of doubts: 'Is it true that God has forbidden . . .?' (Gen. 3:1). For Orthodoxy, the *articulus stantis vel cadentis ecclesiae* is the completeness, inviolability and unchangeability of its foundation in the faith of the Ecumenical Councils of the Ancient Church. Despite the Toronto Statement, Orthodoxy must suffer grievously from the ecumenical claim which increasingly qualifies the absoluteness of this view of itself. Some Orthodox theologians, therefore — there are militant fundamentalists everywhere in the world, inside and outside the churches, — were in the mood to break out from the ecumenical prison. They monotonously recited their formulas, in the way that was usual right back at the beginning of the ecumenical movement, when no common declaration was complete without its Orthodox counter-declaration. It was vexing, admittedly; yet it was also understandable. It is easier to understand it today than it was even a short while back. Protestants find it easier to live with pluralism. They have had more practice. But the ecumenical whirlpool must seem a little diabolical to the Orthodox sometimes, as if 'everything is falling apart'.

There was one very revealing episode. A representative of the Orthodox right wing, one of the angriest and most anxious of them, stood up and said: 'The unity of the Church is not a still-unsolved problem. It was settled by the Councils. According to Orthodox doctrine, the unity of the Church rests on . . .', and he went on to list (if I counted correctly) seven criteria, any one of which, taken seriously, would put an end to ecumenical discussion. As the speaker sat down, a Pentecostal leader from Latin America said to his neighbour: 'He's right. But what he was describing was how we Pentecostal churches see ourselves!'

When everything seems to be falling apart, fundamentalism is a unifying bond between all those who need firm ground to stand on, even between Pentecostalists and Orthodox.

3. Next the *new praxis* — the experiments with structures, life-styles and working methods appropriate to the contemporary missionary situation being conducted in very similar ways by all the churches of all confessions — also makes it seem as if the spirit of an arbitrary modernism, an attitude of nervous defensiveness which is willing to try anything at least to appear up-to-date, has already corrupted the churches, without exception. Their praxis only *seems* to be ecumenical because they have all of them merely copied the ways of the candy-floss culture and followed current fashions.

The difficlty with this criticism is that there is more than a grain of truth in it! There is no denying that modernism has produced some unlovely fruits in the churches. Nor can it be denied that, in the absence of any critical analysis, modernism turns out to be largely sheer defensiveness, a strategy of 'keeping up with the Joneses'. Experiments with forms of worship, for example, undoubtedly encourages the mass production of pure rubbish. Church experiments undoubtedly in some cases produce the kind of pastor who simply swaps the classic patterns of language and conduct for modern ones and is never happier than when no longer regarded as a pastor. It is undeniable that almost the only thing that the flood of new Bible translations has accomplished so far has been a complete break with traditional piety. The list could be extended indefinitely. The new praxis is certainly more than just modernism but it certainly encourages the development of modernism. And modernism is a sell-out.

4. All this inevitably casts a shadow over the fourth factor, the *'existing fellowship'* of the ecumenical movement. Theoretically, there is a world of difference between an ecumenical 'Be kind to each other!' and the fellowship of free people invoked in the study 'Unity of the Church — Unity of Mankind'. But in practice, it is very difficult to draw the dividing line. There is also another kind of fellowship, one not nourished by the power of love but based on the exhaustion of identities, a coexistence in impotence. No doubt, this is preferable to persistent conflict but it soon melts away once aggressiveness begins to build up again.

I must stress the fact that I am not of the opinion that the above interpretation of the factors affecting the ecumenical consensus is a more likely one than other more constructive views. But it does have some basis in ecumenical realities. And when we are dealing with the character and the weight of the Faith and Order consensus, its ambivalent features cannot be omitted. What are the basic underlying drives of this accord?

VII

The most important factor has still to be mentioned. It will be the subject of the next chapter. It is the main question which arises out of the discussion on 'Unity of the Church — Unity of Mankind': Has not the battle line in the struggle for the truth which led to the disintegration of the Church now shifted to a completely different front?

The strategy adopted in Faith and Order was the strategy of 'staging the conflict'. The unsatisfactory character of the Life and Work slogan — 'doctrine divides, service unites' — became apparent once one began seriously to envisage the reunion of Christendom. What Faith and Order decided to tackle and thrash out was precisely the causes of division.

But supposing it turned out that 'faith' and 'order' were no longer the really divisive issues between the churches? Supposing the *real* reason why the peace for which Faith and Order had struggled so strenuously was now a possibility was that there was no longer any real conflict on the fronts on which it had concentrated hitherto? What if the potential source of conflict had meanwhile shifted to quite different places? That would mean that the 'peace' achieved by Faith and Order was only a 'ceasefire' on a secondary front, and that the real battle had shifted elsewhere. Sociologists use the term 'emeritus conflict' (Schelsky) for a social conflict which does not simply disappear but continues to smoulder, still shaping the patterns of social life and feeding tensions in society, though only superficially. In the traditional rituals of conflict these 'emeritus conflicts' now express quite a different conflict potential. They have become no more than a game, are no longer a matter of life and death. They still provide a certain orientation, they still help people to distinguish their own group from other groups, but other divisions, or rather, other reasons for divisions are now more important, more decisive in reality.

Many examples could be given. The conflict in Northern Ireland, for instance, is only superficially a conflict between Catholics and Protestants. Deep down there is quite a different struggle going on. Or take the traditional hostility between Bavarians and Prussians in Germany. This still exists but it has become folklore and the waters of Bavarian separatism drive other mills today.

What about the conflicts which Faith and Order has worked at and brought within sight of solution? Could it be that these, too, are 'emeritus conflicts'? If they were, then the

consensus which has been achieved would be conclusive, but
would make no real difference. It would have been a useful
exercise, if only to tidy matters up. But useful only in a
negative sense. Having settled these traditional frontier-
disputes, or shown them to be capable of settlement, one
could turn with renewed energy and determination to conduct
the struggle for truth at where it really matters, where it really
is a life and death struggle. If this *were* the case, then the
melancholy mood in Louvain is easily understood.

I recall an enigmatic exchange with a Faith and Order
stalwart during coffee-break. It concerned an earlier draft —
long before Louvain — of the document on the Eucharist
being debated at Louvain. I said to my friend: 'It's amazing
what progress you've made! But aren't you working on the
consensus of the day before yesterday?' He smiled at me and
said: 'But of course! What did you think?'

For the moment, I don't quite know what to think!

Greetings,

E.L.

Chapter Two

The New Context

or *The Significance of the Ecumenical Movement for the Survival of Mankind.*

'In what sense can one speak of "the unity of mankind"? What has the Church to say about the solidarity of the human race? How is the unity of the Church related to the unity of mankind?' (WCC Documents FO/71:11)

These introductory questions from the study document 'Unity of the Church — Unity of Mankind', which provided the initial stimulus to discussion of the similarly worded theme at the Commission's meeting in Louvain, seem very restrained and hesitant, almost naïve even, as if in the pursuit of its ecclesiological studies Faith and Order had accidentally stumbled across a new theme, one of many which had always had a place in Christian tradition and in theological reflection on this tradition and were now awaiting their turn for critical study in the context of ecumenical theology.

But appearances are deceptive. Since the study programme was formulated in 1968 it had again and again been insisted, with great emphasis, that work on this theme fell within the *official* tasks covered by the Commission's mandate. That in itself was a warning signal. For example, one of the preparatory papers for the Louvain discussion, based on extensive preliminary work in the member churches, stated: 'The theme belongs to those questions which *need to be raised* in the Faith and Order movement. The purpose of the

Commission is set down in the Constitution as follows: "to proclaim the essential oneness of the Church of Christ and to keep prominently before the Churches of the World Council of Churches the obligation to manifest that unity and its urgency for world mission and evangelism". . . . This has been the task of the Faith and Order movement from the very beginning. But unity also signifies that the Church should be a sign of true communion (*koinonia*) in this divided world. The need to fulfil this task is seen to be particularly urgent today. We are not in fact concerned with a new task, but with a different aspect of the same task. The problem of the unity of the Church should be raised from the point of view of the present world situation. A few selected issues in contemporary life will be examined in the light of the Commission's *official mandate* and then, conversely, the question will be asked what insights can be obtained concerning the task of "proclaiming the oneness of the Church of Jesus Christ" by thinking about it in this new context' (FO/71:11, p. 1. Only in duplicated form).

Moreover, the liveliness of the discussion in Louvain made it quite obvious that this was more than a straightforward addition to the agenda. John Meyendorff's introductory address was a determined effort, almost a last-ditch attempt, to push the theme back into the old framework of the problem.[26] But he was at once opposed, firmly and courteously, by the Latin American Miguez Bonino, who said that in his view there was no going back on the sense of this problem as it had emerged in the ecumenical movement and in the Commission.[27] In the work of the sections, too, it was obvious that an easy accommodation of the old task to the new situation was no solution either. No section could escape the gravitational pull of its own theme. To take the section themes seriously meant setting the problem of church unity in a new and, for most of the participants, unfamiliar light. Unity now meant something materially different from what it had meant before. Almost inevitably, therefore, in a plenary session towards the end of the conference, the question of competence was raised, as it invariably is in church discussions nowadays. What was the essential task of Faith and Order? By choosing this new theme and making it the main theme, had there not already been a break with the traditional understanding and the traditional mandate of Faith and Order?

There were plenty of indications, therefore, that the choice of this theme for the Louvain meeting meant that something more fundamental had happened than appeared at first sight, perhaps more fundamental than even the organizers had intended.

In fact, it was difficult to resist the impression that a shift was taking place at three levels, a threefold 'readaptation':

'Unity of the Church' is not just *a* Faith and Order theme but *the* Faith and Order theme. But this theme was being set in a context which changed its very character. That was the first level.

Then appeared an even more momentous shift. The source of the compulsion to set the old theme in a new context was a changed concept of the Church. The question of the *nature* of the Church receded into the background and the question of the Church's *function* came to the fore. But this focus on the Church's function necessarily involved a 'readaptation' of the Church which, while not conflicting with the *tradition*, clearly shifted the emphasis within the traditional spectrum of concepts of the Church (in the New Testament, for example) and, by doing so, created a noticeable tension with historical *traditions*, with the fully developed ecclesiologies of the 'catholic' wing and also, to an almost equal degree, with the models which had long determined the praxis of the 'protestant' wing of the ecumenical movement.

But the shift was also noticeable at a third level, too: that of the task of Faith and Order as such. Here, too, it seemed, a 'readaptation' was taking place. The 'negative consensus' already achieved, or shown to be capable of being achieved, was not only not adequate but also of dubious importance. It was necessary for Faith and Order, therefore, to reformulate its task and revise its strategy.

Reasons for doing so could also be found in what may be called 'ecumenical politics'. Since Geneva 1966, substantial minorities and even majorities among ordinary members of the churches belonging to the WCC had been disturbed by the way the focus of attention in the ecumenical movement had 'shifted' into the area of social ethics with a view to radical social change. Was the real basis for the Church's existence — its relationship with God, the 'vertical' dimension — in danger of being neglected in the interest of the 'horizontal' dimension — the Church's responsibilities to the world? Was the abnormal concentration on ethics merely a cover-up for the theologians' retreat from their proper task, namely, responsible Christian discourse about God, admittedly a very difficult one? Was not the ecumenical movement in imminent danger of dissolving the Gospel into Law? Theology into anthropology? Schismatic developments were the danger here.

It was necessary, therefore, to give ecumenical theology in the narrower sense a vigorous push into the very centre of the work of the World Council of Churches, institutionally and visibly. But the only way to do this was to incorporate into the traditional Faith and Order agenda the decisive themes of the ecumenical movement, themes which it was not free to pick and choose but were those pressed upon it as a matter of urgency by the changing world and by the situation of the churches in that changing world. In other words, it could only happen if Faith and Order, while not of course monopolizing theology, nevertheless became much more solidly than before the 'theological department' of the World Council of Churches. In his greetings to the Louvain conference, Dr. Eugene Carson Blake, then General Secretary of the WCC, also pointed very explicitly in this direction.

It is reasonable to assume that the new theme, while having substantial arguments in its favour, was also in fact being used as a lever for this 'readaptation', not just tactically, probably not even consciously, but instinctively following the logic of ecumenical advance. And it was at this level that Louvain, in the matter of its main theme, was most successful.

1. *Theme*

In the original study document, four reasons were offered for choosing this theme and making it the main theme.

(*a*) It was contemporary. The world today is marked by a growing global interdependence of all people, all groups and social processes. At the same time, this interdependence multiplies the possibilities of conflict and the dangers of catastrophic developments.

(*b*) The churches had accepted this situation of interdependence — fraught as it is with the possibilities of conflict — as a 'challenge', to use the ecumenical jargon. At Uppsala especially their response had been to give fresh currency to the original Christian axiom of the 'unity of mankind' before God. But the many problems raised by this proposed connection between social interdependence and the unity of mankind as traditionally understood by Christians were a challenge to theological reflection, especially on the matter of responsible action by the churches in secular conflicts. In other words, what was needed was theological reflection on social ethics. 'What should be the Church's attitude in the new situation? . . . How could it become a force for true community?'

'True community'! Thus, right at the very outset, one of the key phrases which would prove decisive for the study itself and for the discussions in Louvain was uttered. It indicated the theological and ethical difference between the reality of interdependence and the Christian notion of the unity of mankind. It therefore pointed to the open space for the preaching and the action of the churches — to their 'marching orders'. But when this keyword 'true community' was applied to the growing interdependence of the human race as both condemnation and promise, it soon backfired on the churches themselves. How did they themselves measure up to this 'true community'? And this question had to be put not simply as an exercise in self-criticism but rather in order to provoke the churches to a new understanding of themselves. 'How must the Church *understand* itself and what *form* must it take if it is really to be able to fulfil its mission?'

(*c*) The growing interdependence of the world constituted a very radical test for the Church. Hitherto it had spoken of the 'unity of mankind' mainly in two senses: from an eschatological standpoint and from an ecclesiological standpoint. The unifying of mankind — not abstractly but in the reality of the peace already established — is one of the aspects of the kingdom of God which has 'drawn near' in Jesus Christ. And this peace, too, like salvation itself, is anticipated in the Church. In the eschatological tension between the 'not yet' and the 'but already', the Church *is* 'the

unity of mankind' in the form in which this is realizable now
in this penultimate age. 'The Church is bold to speak of itself
as the sign of the coming unity of mankind' (*Uppsala Report*, p.
20).

The more contemporary world society becomes
interdependent and the more the possibilities of conflict
multiply, the more double-edged this traditional affirmation
becomes. It acquires the overtones of a declaration of intent
which are missing in the traditional usage. Does the Church
have any programme for solving the problem of the survival of
mankind in this process of growing interdependence? Is it a
model, an instrument, an active agent in this complex event?
If it is, it will certainly be drawn into controversy with other
programmes, other models, other agents advancing a similar
claim.

(*d*) Since the Church itself was being interrogated about its
business, its nature and self-understanding, it was also
impossible for Faith and Order to evade the new set of
problems. Admittedly this implied a shift of emphasis but 'the
Commission on Faith and Order, in the course of recent
years, has been led more and more to the study of *the calling
and mission of the Church in the contemporary world*'.

The document described how the problem had shifted in
the period between Montreal 1963 and Bristol 1967.
Formulations creep in here which suffice to show the 'forward
leap' which had taken place in ecumenical studies and in the
work of Faith and Order. If the Commission 'is truly to serve
the Church, it must be ready to do so at the points where the
Church is most exposed. To attempt this would in itself be to
promote Christian unity'. This quotation from the Aarhus
minutes recalls the Life and Work argument. This impression
deepens when the study document continues: '. . . the
common clarification of important contemporary problems
will indirectly help to draw the churches together.' But this in
fact is how Faith and Order now speaks. In other words, the
Commission at least faced the possibility that its traditional
strategy — the strategy of 'staging' the interconfessional
conflict — would now have to be changed, or at least
extended. The study document sharpened its question
precisely in this direction: 'In studying the *role* of the Church

in relation to the unity of mankind, its purpose is to contribute indirectly to opening up the way *to the unity of the Church'*. The new emphasis on the *function* of the Church is quite unmistakable here. It is still the old aim — 'to open the way to the unity of the Church' — but by a new method — the study of the role of the church for the survival of mankind.

2. *The Importance of Louvain*

'This is a discussion among amateurs', commented an American Jesuit who, like the author, was attending Louvain as an observer.

He was right in two respects. Both inside and outside the ecumenical movement, the problems of 'social justice', 'dialogue', 'racism', the 'socially marginalized', 'religion and culture', were and are being studied more competently and fruitfully in many other places than in Faith and Order. Colleagues from Church and Society, the Programme to Combat Racism, the Department of World Mission and Evangelism, can hardly have learned or experienced anything specially new in Louvain.

But even in its own special field of ecumenical theology — particularly that of ecclesiology — the Commission's discussions did not rise much above the amateur level. The old themes had now to be studied from a new angle, with new assumptions, and on the basis of data which was new both in substance and in kind. People were not yet used to this. Tried and tested competence in the traditional materials seemed challenged all of a sudden. The Faith and Order 'professionals' seemed to be reduced to the level of 'beginners' — novices at the very game they had themselves invented!

But this was exactly what Louvain was: a 'beginning', a long prepared, far from arbitrary, even indispensable yet nonetheless disturbing 'shift' on the part of the Faith and Order Commission in the direction of Church and Society, in the direction of the new ecumenical programmes and their theological reflections and responsibilities, and, at the same time, a 'forward leap' in Faith and Order's understanding of itself and in its strategy. The *old* question of 'what no longer divides' was still important. But the *new* question — one which had never been so central in the Commission's studies before — was 'What is to be done together' for the world *and* for the reunion of Christendom, neither one without the other?

The Double Inversion

The truth of that becomes all the plainer if we look at the whole process in perspective. We then discover that it has the pattern of a complicated fugue. First there is a theme, which is then developed in counterpoint; then an inversion of the theme and even an inversion of this inversion. But the outcome of this double inversion, this game of mirrors, is not a return to the situation as it was at the outset, but an enhancement of the whole process with a new quality.

In a semi-official account of the discussions in Louvain, John Deschner offers the following interpretation: 'The four years of work embraces an easily-overlooked shift in approach which partly accounts for the tentativeness with which this report ends. The preparatory stages and opening statements sighted most of the underlying issues and stated them with greater clarity than the subsequent Louvain discussions. But Louvain contributed a wealth of material enrichment and insight and, in its frequent warnings, an important dialectical control upon any theological triumphalism about this theme' (*Louvain*, p. 198). That is obviously an understatement. What actually happened?

At the beginning, in the study document published in 1969, we had rather confident affirmations about the ecumenical movement and a set of questions which betrayed a somewhat arrogant sense of the Church's mission and task in relation to the need of mankind for unity. 'What function does the Church have, in the light of the will of God, to lead the world to unity?' Next the study document examined the scope of statements describing the Church 'as sign of the coming unity of mankind', ending with an interpretation of the possible role of Christendom in the development of mankind — put in the form of a question, of course, but so emphatically that some might have thought it a bit fraudulent: 'How can the Church become a factor and even a worker (*faber*) in the historical process?' It spoke of the need for 'prophetic planning', ventured to ask whether the Church could produce its own 'patterns of community life', viewed world Christendom as a 'coherent militant community' consecrated to the struggle to

clear 'obstacles to freedom and community' out of the way,
and concluded with a vision of the global church community,
girding and equipping itself for radical witness.

This draft was first of all criticized on theological grounds,
and the criticisms increased in sharpness right down to
Louvain and at Louvain itself, in the addresses of Kohnstamm and Meyendorff. But the focus of the theological
criticism was not the centrality of the Church for human
destiny. What was emphasized far more was the eschatological proviso. Pessimism as to the possibilities of
human development within history deepened. The principal
role of the Church was seen again in terms of its eucharistic
presence rather than in terms of its active intervention in the
world.

The page was turned at Louvain when the work in the
sections began, if not sooner. Stored up in the realities of
interdependence is a potential for conflict of such grotesque
dimensions that any large claims for the Church simply die on
our lips. When, for example, in the first two sessions of
Section IV, the concept of 'marginalization' began to take on
flesh and blood for us when we were shown a documentary
film on the *leper minority* (already in the Bible they constituted
the classic group of the marginalized, and still today
constitute an army of millions of people carefully excluded
from normal life in society not because they are contagious
but because people are afraid of them); or again, when a man
in a wheelchair, a victim of infantile paralysis, began to speak
to us of his experiences of polite disrespect and false pity —
then anything else we might want to say would first have to be
tested against such realities as these.

When 'racism' ceases to be a mere word and becomes men
and women around a table giving their own personal
testimony to the way in which racism in the world and in the
Church has ruined their own lives and that of their children, it
becomes quite impossible to offer merely verbal theological
answers, as the ecumenical movement has tried so long to do.

It became impossible, therefore, to simply proceed with the
agenda as planned. It was impossible to put the direct
question as to the Church's role in the struggle for the unity of
mankind on which man's survival in an interdependent world
depends. There were prior questions: Into what situation does

the situation of mankind bring the Church? What part is played in Christianity, in the churches, in the ecumenical movement by the world's conflict potential? In short, the theme was turned right round. It now read: '*Unity of Mankind — Unity of the Church*'. In plain terms: 'How did the division of mankind and mankind's efforts to achieve unity influence the division of the Church and its efforts towards reunion?'

Human Unity — Church Unity

But when the question is turned round in this way it is even more difficult for the world to accept the Church's emphasis on its own self-understanding and on its programmes for world development. For what divides the world divides the Church, the Church especially. Even the Church is invaded by the *global class struggle* where questions are asked about 'justice', equality of opportunity, the redistribution of power and resources. For example, it divides the Church into a tiny group of donor churches and a large group of receiving churches. It imposes a paternalistic attitude on the donor churches and forces the receiving churches into the ambivalent attitude of the poor, who would rather repel the hand that feeds them because besides feeding them it also humiliates them. And this is only the tip of the ecumenical iceberg. The class division runs right through the Church. And so far as the 'social question' is concerned, every single one of the churches has a skeleton — indeed many skeletons — in its cupboard, beginning with the failure of Christendom on the slavery question during the first Christian millennium. Nor is it merely a matter of Christendom having unfortunately been unable to escape completely from social influences. It has been common knowledge, since Max Weber at the very latest, that the secular spirit of total production and growth is indirectly a derivative of the Christian spirit. The churches have not just been the victims of world disorder, they have in many respects been themselves the wellspring of the disorder which subsequently destroys their own unity.

And this could be illustrated from every one of the themes tackled in the sections at Louvain. The *pluralism* of religions, world views and ideologies which makes 'dialogue' a *sine qua non* of survival is partly the consequence of the spread of western civilization over the whole world, partly the result of its own domestic secularism. *Racism* is not only a divisive element among human beings in general, it is and always has been a central problem in the history of the Church and theology, from the unhealthy particularism of late Judaism and its mirror image in the hostility of the ancient world to Judaism, traces of which are (as is well known) still detectable in the New Testament, right down to *apartheid* in South Africa which has been furnished with a theological basis and systematized by the dominant church in that country. The marginalization of sizable social groups not only has a long history even in the Church but, from a sociological standpoint, is today especially characteristic of church milieus which are particularly stubborn in excluding anything that is different from 'us' and even casts doubts on it from a moral or religious standpoint. Finally, the question as to how far *culture* had not only been influenced by but also in turn itself influenced Christianity, sometimes making it parochial almost to vanishing point, was in fact the main theme assigned to Section V at Louvain.

What divides the world also divides the Church. In part this is a kind of byproduct of the influence of Christianity; in some cases, the divisive element would not have been there without the auxiliary influence of religion in, for example, the education of the conscience; in other cases, it has been the Church which also simply finds itself incapable of excluding the divisive factor and controlling it at least within its own borders.

From this angle, the question still needing to be answered is whether the divisive power which influences the church from the society in which it lives affects only the *bene esse* of the Church or its *esse*. If it 'only' affects the *bene esse*, this means to say that the Church does not even have the power to transform social antagonisms into fruitful tensions in its own domestic life. But in that case, how could it possibly have the power to overcome them in the world or even help to overcome them? The very lowest target for the Church in that case would be renewal, radical renewal, if and because, despite its parlous condition, it still trusts more in the Gospel of reconciliation by which it lives than it gives the impression of doing.

On the other hand, if the divisive effect of social

antagonisms *within* the Church touches the very *esse* of the Church, then it cannot simply be a question of greater fidelity on the part of the Church to what it believes. In that case, the question it has to ask itself is whether in these matters it has not up to the present been mistaken in what it believed; whether in this new world situation it has not discovered something heretical within itself which up to now it has either simply not noticed or else tolerated against its better judgement. In other words, faced with the possibilities of conflict in the world and the influence of these possibilities on the Church itself, the question is whether the Church as it now exists, really *is* the Church.

In some at least of the problems dealt with in the sections, it is open to dispute whether it was simply a matter of the *bene esse* and therefore a question of renewal, or a matter of the *esse* and therefore a question of institutional repentance and a necessary surgical operation on the substance of traditional doctrine and order. If it is true that 'the Christ of the eucharist and the Christ of the poor are one and the same Christ', then what is really at stake in this indissoluble connection between sacramental understanding and practice, on the one hand, and the principle of social justice, as the indisputable standard for the domestic ordering of the Church and for its action in the world, on the other, is not simply the degree of the Church's credibility but the reality of the Church as Church. So far as racism within the Church is concerned, the problem of Judaism in the New Testament is undoubtedly an anticipation of this issue and we all know that Paul's judgement was that what was at stake here was Gospel or no Gospel, and therefore salvation or no salvation.

But discussion on this question is not yet over. Even if it were 'only' a matter of obedience and credibility and not of the very faith of the Church, that would still be serious enough. To be in a position to help the world, the ecumenical movement would have to ask whether, in face of the state of our world, it can *itself* be helped and, if so, in what way? It would have to explain the reasons for its hopeful assumption that it could make a contribution to the unity of mankind, considering its previous failure to resist the forces of division within its own borders. *Hic Rhodus, hic salta!* That would then have been the first news out of Louvain.

The double inversion would follow from that. The Church had been 'bold' to speak of itself as a sign of the future unity of mankind, but before it can be such a sign it has first to be stripped of all its pretensions and shown up as a very manifest sign of the present *disunity* of mankind. *Not* indeed — and this is most important — because of its confessional divisions, but for quite different reasons.

The Sign of Division as Promise of Peace

But surely this permits us to ask — if not quite so euphorically — whether the Church could not perhaps show domestically how, on the basis of the fact of Christ, the divisive factor loses its force, or at any rate its power to dehumanize and endanger the world, and how, through union with Christ, human development can succeed in spite of it. If everything which tears the world apart is visible in the Church as in a *distorting mirror*, could anything be more important than that the world should experience here, in the Church, where the division is so obvious and felt to be especially inconsistent because it contradicts so sharply all our fine words, the chaos being reduced, an order of common life struggling to birth in which differences are not met with hostility and threatened with destruction but held together in fruitful exchange and mutual development?

Everything depends on taking as realistic a view of the situation as possible. What divides the world also divides the Church. That should not surprise us. The Church is part of the world, a segment of humanity. It is 'believing humanity' (Dantine)[28] or it is nothing. The only difference between Church and mankind, ultimately, is a 'pneumatological' one, the difference made by faith as the work of the Holy Spirit. But this is a difference which is not at our disposal; the Church cannot take it over and manage it, cannot translate it into its structures. What divides the world will certainly not lose its divisive force in the passage between world and Church.

But its meaning changes. It becomes — in good ecumenical jargon — a 'challenge'. Not just a challenge to diaconia but a challenge to faith. Put simply, it should not be so in the Church, or at any rate should not remain so. The Church should *not* be a helpless victim of racism, for example. Marginalized people should *not* be left on the margin of the

Church and made even more marginal than before.

We have to realize that in these cases it is not a matter of divisions which, like confessional divisions, can arise in, or at least have some connection with, the struggle for truth. In fact there is no difference among Christians on the question of racism. Even the Boer churches have now admitted that 'racism is sin'. Nor is there any disagreement on the question of marginalization. All Christians know that, in the sight of Jesus, the marginal people are central. And all Christians agree that there will be no racial divisions or marginalization in the kingdom of God for which they all long, even if they differ widely in their understanding of it. What is not possible is that this should not be anticipated in practice, at least within the Church whose highest calling is to be a *foretaste* of this kingdom, to live its life as an *anticipation* of this kingdom, to the very best of its ability. Diaconia, missionary preaching, or the Church's dealings with the world around it, these do not yet even enter the picture. *Here* it is the integrity of the faith and of the Church itself which is at stake. Here it is a question of how wide the gap between what is believed and what can be seen, between what the Church is meant to be and what its structures and praxis actually are, can be allowed to become before we face a situation of crisis in respect of faith and piety.

The Crisis of Faith

Racist church structures and the tolerence of marginalization in organized church life *do in fact* represent a situation of crisis for faith. The Christian could no longer live with himself if he did not try to change things here. And all Christians are in principle agreed on this. There is no conflict here. The deepest interest of Christians constrains them to try, at least in the Church itself, to conquer racism and marginalization as they believe this *can* be done, and to eliminate them from the structures and praxis of the Church as far as possible. It is as simple as that.

But in doing this, in seeking to be a militant anticipation of the coming kingdom in this situation of crisis for faith, the Church also becomes something in the nature of an experiment, a *model* for interdependent humanity which, because of the pent-up conflict potential in its situation, faces the choice: unite or perish! This, too, is a basically simple situation. So long as no alternatives are visible, people will tend to accept the dangerous *status quo* fatalistically. But once an alternative appears, fatalism evaporates. People begin to gain some relief from the pressures to which they had previously yielded. They begin to play with possibilities, to test alternatives. The learning process begins in the interplay of action and reflection.

It is not really important here whether the alternatives envisaged arise out of special conditions (e.g. in the case of the Church, the crisis for faith). The alternative models of society in capitalism and communism influence each other, stimulate each other, keep each other fluid, even though they are incompatible. Or to take an example closer to the Church, the world religions are in competition with each other, the confessions within Christianity are in competition with each other, whether they like it or not. Once an alternative hoves in sight, it is impossible to escape the learning process. However strange the alternative may appear, the fact is that, from now on, one's own solution, one's own uncomfortable *status quo*, is only relative. Fatalism, a naïve fatalism at any rate, will no longer do.

The Church has demonstrably operated again and again — often quite involuntarily — as an alternative of this kind, as a disturbing element within society. It has introduced ideas — e.g. the equality of all men before God, the idea of responsibility, etc. — which have promoted emancipation even where the Church itself was unwilling to interpret them in an explicitly liberating sense. It has tried out models — the model of general mass education, for example — which were designed exclusively to serve the Church's own interests but which nevertheless acquired a social impetus of their own. A Church which produces ideas and invents models which — first of all in the Church because of the crisis of faith — demonstrate in one way or other how people can live constructively with the conflict-potential in this inter-dependent world, is bound in the end to be also a *ferment* for social change. In the end it is really the same people working at learning processes and union experiments within the Church who then, within society, find themselves dealing with similar problems. When, as citizens, they find themselves under the pressure of an unsatisfactory *status quo*, they will not be able to forget that there is an alternative.

After this double inversion, the Louvain theme now reads: *the crisis in the Church and the crisis of mankind*. It is clear from this that the ecumenical movement cannot stop short at the realization that the divisions of mankind are also operative within the Church, that faith is therefore confronted with a crisis, begins to defend itself, and by doing so successfully, certainly will also produce models and resources for the union of mankind. Once the social relevance of active faith is really understood, theology and the Church cannot possibly let the matter rest there. Theology and the Church must accept responsibility for this social relevance of active faith and incorporate it in their own plans and changes. For the Church is, in fact, an instrument of God's saving work in the world and exists for the sake of the world. It has always known and believed this and always said this. The only difference is that this 'existence for the sake of the world' is now seen to be far more complex than it had seemed when world history was considered, both in theory and in practice, as no more than the overture to the Last Day. The fact that the Church exists and is what it is, the fact that it works and the way in which it works — negatively and positively — is important for the world, not just eschatologically but also historically and socially. The Church cannot possibly go on behaving, therefore, as if this social dimension did not exist. It has to be tackled responsibly in the way the Church acts.

To this extent, therefore, the way the study document formulated the question proves wholly justified in this third turn. But the detour via Louvain was quite indispensable. In fact, this detour has not yet been travelled, only discovered. One of the ecumenical movement's earliest 'declarations of intent' was the call: 'Let the Church be the Church!' (Edinburgh 1910). Even after Louvain, especially after Louvain, that call still holds good. Only it has taken on a more critical momentum. Let the Church be the Church! Let the Church become the Church in the way it deals with what really divides and endangers it because it also divides and endangers mankind. Let the Church demonstrate that it is the Church. Only in this way can it do anything for the unity of mankind.

Chapter Three

The Handmaid of the Churches

or *The Inconclusiveness of the Ecumenical Movement*

The Faith and Order Commission is only one of the ecumenical movement's fields of activity. Everything happens much more quietly and unobtrusively there than elsewhere. Yet it is in some ways the heart and conscience of the ecumenical movement. For its specific goal is the union of Christendom, and this is ultimately the goal of all the departments of the World Council of Churches, the Council's *raison d'être*. The others pursue this same goal in different ways. For some, unity is a means rather than an end in itself — an indispensable requirement for mission, development aid, diakonia, the witness of the Church in world politics: an essential presupposition if full credibility is to be restored to Christendom and its full potential developed. For others, unity is the ultimate goal, one which can only be attained, however, by uniting now in the service of world development and in mission. They attach a different importance to unity and adopt a different strategy.

Nevertheless, for the work of all the departments, the decisive criterion is the union of Christendom. In all that they do they must satisfy the following questions: Do they do justice to the given unity of the Church as attested in the New Testament? Do they really express this unity? Do they help the churches to advance towards the restoration of their

visible, complete and unrestricted fellowship? For all
expressions of the ecumenical movement, the central biblical
passage is and remains John 17:21. On his way to the cross,
the Johannine Christ prayed: 'May they all be one: as thou,
Father, art in me, and I in thee, so also may they be in us, that
the world may believe that thou didst send me.'

Visible Unity

In the last analysis, the work of Faith and Order is quite
simply and exclusively an exegesis of this passage, an attempt
to answer this prayer. It thus keeps the whole ecumenical
movement oriented towards this goal. It was natural,
therefore, for the Central Committee, when seeking to
reformulate the functions and aims of the World Council of
Churches, to ask the help of the Commission in drafting the
first and all-important sentence.

A good deal can be learned from a brief account of how the
Commission acquitted itself of this task. The existing
constitution of the WCC provided the starting point. It did
not include any definition of aims and functions at all, as
such. Section III (i) simply referred to the original founding
movements: the aim of the WCC was 'to carry on the work of
the two world movements for Faith and Order and for Life
and Work, as also that of the International Missionary
Council'. In the Faith and Order Commission's own
constitution — which naturally provided part of the
immediate background for the redefinition of the WCC's
objectives — we find the following definition: 'to proclaim the
essential oneness of the Church of Christ and to keep
prominently before the World Council and the churches the
obligation to manifest that unity and its urgency for world
mission and evangelism'. This formulation resulted from the
integration of the International Missionary Council in the
WCC in 1961.

The very fact that the WCC was now formulating aims and
functions focussed on specific goals was itself an indication
that it had meanwhile become something more than the sum
of its parent organizations. It had itself become an essential
expression and key instrument of the 'existing fellowship' of
the churches. It needed to explain the aims of this fellowship,
therefore. It is significant that, whereas hitherto no such

attempt had been made to define functions in relation to aims, so as to avoid putting the churches under pressure, now after a bare quarter of a century it was clearly felt to be necessary to nail the colours to the mast. The objectives of the first stage had been achieved: the integration of the pioneer movements, the creation of an international instrument of cooperation in all fields, and a common mind among the churches. What was the way ahead?

In its own new draft of the constitution, the Central Committee defined the aim as follows: 'To keep before the churches the goal of unity in one faith and in one eucharistic fellowship and to foster the progressive manifestation of this unity and the expression in worship of our common life in Christ' (*Minutes*, p. 46). As stated here, the goal was unity in one faith and in one eucharistic fellowship. The function of the WCC was to keep this goal before the churches (which in fact implies a certain anticipatory visibility in the ecumenical movement, as is also shown by the end of the sentence, which implies that the 'common life in Christ' is something already given which still needs to be expressed in worship) and to facilitate and foster progress in the demonstration of this unity.

The Commission did not accept this draft and proposed an alternative version: 'To call the churches to the goal of visible unity in one faith and in one eucharistic fellowship expressed in worship and in common life in Christ and to advance towards that unity in order that the world may believe' (*Minutes*, p. 46). This was at once bolder and much more cautious.

Bolder, because the goal here is *visible* unity in one faith and in one eucharistic fellowship, expressed in worship and in common life in Christ. Certainly the rearrangement of what the Central Committee's draft contained leads now to a certain redundancy: it was not really necessary to say that eucharistic fellowship must be expressed liturgically! But what Faith and Order wanted to do was to sharpen the goal. It was from start to finish a matter of visibility, which undoubtedly also includes its structural expression. Hence, too, the stress on the fact that 'common life in Christ' is more than the oft-invoked 'existing fellowship'. It cannot be regarded as our starting point, something already achieved, only needing to find expression. It is itself still the goal.

Moreover, the World Council was not merely to keep the goal before the churches but to 'call' them to it. It is not simply an instrument but also a prod to the churches. It has a prophetic task of its own.

But the inclination to caution in the new definition is even more important. The progress the Central Committee wanted to facilitate and foster, the assumption being that it was somehow already happening, was something for which the member churches and they alone were responsible. The WCC has nothing to facilitate and foster here. Its business is to call them to advance. Unless the churches themselves advance, there is no progress, no real progress, anyhow.

Perhaps all this is over-subtle. But ecumenical theologians are usually extremely careful in their formulations. Their success depends on their walking warily. At least their intention was quite plain: the WCC was to stick to its traditional role and remain a prod to the churches, nothing more, nothing less. It was not to water down or reduce the goal. And it was to saddle the churches firmly with their unique responsibility. International cooperation had largely been achieved. 'Existing fellowship' had been achieved even if its ecclesiological significance for the guidance of the churches remained unformulated. Progress had been achieved therefore, but not in the essentials, only in the realm of possibilities. It was now up to the member churches.

All this, of course, also had some bearing on ecumenical politics. Among others, it was also ultimately a question of — Rome. And for Rome a unity which is not at the same time a structural unity is quite inconceivable. At the same time, however, any transfer of the initiative, in however restricted a sense, to some other level above the Holy See and the 'corresponding' authorities in the other confessional families (if such exist) is just as inconceivable. Yet this in no way detracts from the insight provided by this part of the Louvain agenda. Indeed it strengthens it. It was not simply considerations of 'principle' which led Faith and Order to insist on both greater boldness *and* caution, but because in ecumenical praxis nothing else will really do.

Let me now try to examine, in the light of this, the ambiguous question posed in the original sub-title of my book with reference to the ecumenical movement as a whole. 'What moves the Ecumenical Movement?' Louvain will serve here simply as an illustration. What drives the ecumenical movement? And what does it accomplish? What does it achieve? The answer to both these questions must be derived, not from first principles, but from the actual state of the ecumenical movement, not from its programme but from its praxis.

The question in the book title was deliberately ambiguous; what moves the ecumenical movement *and* what does the ecumenical movement move? The sub-title of this third chapter is also ambiguous: 'The *Inconclusiveness* of the Ecumenical Movement'. The present state of the ecumenical process permits no unambiguous conclusions. And the reason for this is that the movement itself is irresolute, that the member churches themselves are irresolute. New resolves are overdue yet the churches hang back, indecisive, hesitant and afraid. It may be that these required decisions are simply not possible, not yet possible, or even for ever impossible. So that the answer to the ambiguous question in the book title can itself only be an ambiguous one.

1. *Indecision about Goals*

From the very beginning, the ecumenical movement has never really been certain of its goals. The main reason for this is that quite different and even conflicting motives have been operating.

In the 'Call to the Churches' issued by the inaugural Assembly in Amsterdam in 1948, it was stated: 'Our first and deepest need is not new organization but the renewal, or rather the rebirth of the actual churches.' Since then the indissoluble connection between 'unity' and 'renewal' has been one of the constant formulas of ecumenical theory and practice. Unity can only come through the renewal of the 'actual churches'. Yet at the same time, unity is itself the ecumenical way to renewal. As the churches are radically renewed, they unite. As they seek unity on the basis of the fundamentals of faith, they are renewed.

Verbally, there has never been much controversy over this. But there has always been controversy over the real meaning of 'radical renewal'. The different confessions are in dispute as

to the meaning of renewal. Since every church considers itself
to be the true Church, or at any rate as the relatively truest
manifestation of the Church of the Christian creeds, and since
this basic conviction is just the one which is not open to
discussion (that is the meaning of the Toronto Statement), the
most obvious way of applying the term in practice was to
think of each of the other churches and to see renewal as
bringing *them* closer and closer into line with one's own form
of ecclesial life. Right up to the time of the Second Vatican
Council, the Roman Catholic Church was quite frankly
unable to think in any other terms than those of the 'return',
the 'home-coming', of the separated Christians, whose
'associations' could not even be called 'churches' — not even
for diplomatic reasons — into the all-embracing bosom of
Rome. The Orthodox Churches did not speak in quite the
same brusque fashion because, even today, their unity is the
conciliar unity of autonomous churches. Their way of saying
the same thing as Rome was to summon the other churches to
return to the Ancient Church consensus of the Seven
Ecumenical Councils. And because of their doctrine, the
Protestant churches make things very much easier for
themselves in this question of radical renewal by basing their
continuity on 'God's Word alone' and by being also prepared,
in principle, to submit their own church forms to the
authority and criticism of this Word. But they also continue to
expect the other churches to do the same and to expose
themselves to this 'Word', which the other churches cannot do
since they insist on the presence of Christ in their church
order, or the presence of the 'enchurched' Word. Even in the
fundamental concepts of the member churches, therefore,
'radical renewal' means something different in each case. All
of them can accept renewal as true repentance on the part of
individual Christians and church functionaries. All of them
can accept that even for themselves as institutions there is a
lost fullness to be recovered. But any change in the basic
pattern is something profoundly unthinkable for any of them.

But it is not only the confessions which differ over 'renewal'.
If anything the dispute is even fiercer among the original
movements which came together to form the World Council.
For Life and Work, renewal is wholly oriented towards the
world: its purpose is to make the Church and all its resources

available for the world in its contradictions and hopelessness. Much the same thing could be said of World Mission and Evangelism. Yet it makes all the difference whether one interprets pro-existence diaconally or in terms of mission and evangelism. Faith and Order, again, thinks of renewal as the restoration of the fullness of biblical faith and *koinonia* and as the recovery of the full credibility and relevance of preaching in the contemporary world.

But these are far from being the only currents. There is also the youth and student movement, within and outside the WCC, which has given and continues to provide the ecumenical movement with its best people and its best ideas. For them, renewal is always translated into the dramas of the generation conflict. Not that they see the renewed Church as the church of the sons in contrast to the fossilized church of the fathers. But for them, the tradition is always primarily the quarry for future forms. For the most part, their idea of renewal is rather vague but its basic mood is utopian, aimed at the achievement of future possibilities rather than at the restoration of a past fullness. And true to past form in the generation conflict, the visions of future possibilities get more and more radical. In terms of social psychology, the theology of revolution is a theology of the young or of the still 'young in heart', a human type with a fairly long history.

There is also the rich variety of lay movements in the ecumenical movement, particularly those inspired by Protestantism. For them, the basic conflict, the conflict in the light of which they project a renewed Church, is that between clergy and people. Fundamentally, and even historically, their motive for renewal is emancipation, a laicizing impulse, though in the case of the domestic church movements the picture is complicated by the fact that as loyal church members they have never really been willing to admit this anti-clerical or critical tendency in their form of renewal and never wished to embody it in their strategy in the church. To the extent that the lay movements then became domesticated and acquired an official status in the churches (one of the smartest strategies of the established churches in countering tendencies critical of the church is precisely such official recognition), the laicizing approach sank back more and more into the unconscious. But when dreams of a renewed Church reawaken, all these suppressed forces of rebellion spring back into play. It is hardly necessary to labour the point that the strong church women's movements are an important form of this unfulfilled and therefore still smouldering rebellion.

But even that is still not the whole story. For the controversy over the meaning of 'radical renewal' deepens more and more as the ecumenical movement advances. It becomes a controversy between the 'younger' churches and the old established churches, between the Third World and the North Atlantic capitals, between the races, between the cultures in which the Christian faith has been implanted, between the world religions (and therefore in an acute form between Latin America and Africa). All the emerging centrifugal forces in the ecumenical movement produce their rival concepts of renewal.

Renewal is, therefore, to put it bluntly, a thoroughly polemical term. If the union of Christendom depends on its 'radical renewal', no wonder the ecumenical movement is still undecided as to its motivations and goals.

This state of affairs was further intensified when in 1948 the ecumenical movement became a movement of the *churches*, with all the ambivalence implicit in this polarization, already amply illustrated in our previous analysis. One can even go so far as to say that by becoming an organization of churches, the ecumenical movement practically ceases to be a renewal movement. I mean that the established churches, the institutions, even discounting for the moment their confessional controversies, are *bound* to understand by 'renewal' something categorically different from the experimental pioneering moves taking place within and around them. Obedient to their mandate and following their own interests, the institutions are *bound* to think of renewal as a more or less radical *reform* of what now exists. But experimental ecumenism is bound to conceive renewal in *revolutionary* terms, or at least in terms extremely critical of institutions — this is part of the inherent logic of their fresh start. In other words, there is an ecumenical version of the perennial conflict between those who advocate changes *within* the system and those who want to *overthrow* the system. And this conflict is proceeding all the time *within* the confessions, *within* the different currents which make up the ecumenical stream, *within* the lay and youth movements, *within* the Geneva departments and their committees, and, finally, between the institutional ecumenical movement with all its inner contradictions and experimental ecumenism at the ground level. The institutions are *bound* to think that renewal is compatible with self-preservation. Their opponents are bound to appeal to the maxim, 'Die to become!' or, in Christian terminology, 'Death and Resurrection'. Ultimately, no compromise is possible here, either in motives or aims.

Everywhere in the movement this dilemma is felt. In Louvain it was, surprisingly enough, actually an Orthodox who voiced the sharpest criticism in this respect, although the widespread impression that the Orthodox are particularly hesitant over the term renewal is largely true. 'During this search for real unity', said Savas Agourides, in his meditation on the future of the ecumenical movement, '. . . in this pilgrimage to the *Una Sancta,* to our goal, the churches are led by two factors: repentance and renewal, on the one hand, and the need for defence *vis-à-vis* the world and its pressures, on the other. My impression is that the second factor is much stronger than the first. It is not necessary to refer here to the new experience of cooperation among the churches during the last two generations. The feeling of common problems and dangers, the process of the unification of the world in many fields, and the need to experiment together and to help each other, have created a kind of unity. . . . The fact that the churches are together is an achievement. . . . This "togetherness" . . . has undoubted positive values . . .; it is, however, an expression of the defence of the churches against the challenge of the modern world. . . . The first danger is to think that this "togetherness" of the churches *vis-à-vis* this world is the unity of the Church for our days and to be content with that. . . . The second danger may come from disappointment at the defensive character of the existing "togetherness" and enthusiasm about contemporary achievements of the world in the creation of community. . . .' (*Minutes,* p. 48).

This was an interesting contribution, not least because it showed the polemical character of the concept of renewal and the interchangeability of the arguments. For everything which is criticized here as defensive under the slogan of 'the

challenge of the world' — the whole range of Church and
Society themes, for example, and ecumenical *diakonia* —
usually appears on the Protestant side as the *avant-garde* thrust
of the ecumenical process. And the quiet work of Faith and
Order, so often dismissed as irrelevant traditionalism by those
who take this world-oriented stance, appears in a different
light as our only possibility of real advance. There could be no
better illustration of the ambiguity of motives and goals.

The Conciliarity Formula

It is against this background that we should see what the
verbal consensus has nevertheless yielded concerning the
concrete goal of the ecumenical movement. On this central
point, there is no disagreement even between the Central
Committee's draft and the Faith and Order Commission's
version. The aim is 'visible unity in the *one* faith and in the *one*
eucharistic fellowship'. And that is no empty formula. Both
elements in the formula point to elaborated concepts and, to
some extent at least, to strategies. Yet the irresolution as to
goals has not been eliminated. Indeed the concepts are so
concrete that this indecision becomes all the more patent.

The concept of 'conciliarity' is really concerned with visible
unity in 'one eucharistic fellowship' and how this can be
achieved. The best of the texts drafted at Louvain dealt with
this theme. [The basis of discussion was a passage from the
report on the unity of the Church formulated and adopted by
the Fourth Assembly in Uppsala.]

'The Uppsala Assembly in 1968 spoke of the World Council
of Churches as a "transitional opportunity for eventually
actualizing a truly universal, ecumenical, conciliar form of
common life" and suggested that the member churches
should "work for the time when a genuinely universal council
may once more speak for all Christians and lead the way into
the future".' Louvain noted that there was, strictly speaking,
a double impulse in the Uppsala proposal: 'Conciliarity' was,
in the first place, 'a permanent *feature* of the Church's life' and,
in the second place, 'an *event* which one day may take place'.
As a structure, conciliarity means 'the coming together of
Christians — locally, regionally or globally — for common
prayer, counsel and decision, in the belief that the Holy Spirit
can use such meetings for his own purpose of reconciling,

renewing and reforming the Church, for guiding it towards the fullness of truth and love' (*Louvain,* p. 226).

That doesn't sound very exciting. The conciliar structure is nothing other than the specifically Christian model of fundamental democracy, a distinctive 'soviet' model. Unity is not organized hierarchically, nor even in a code of timelessly valid truths literally binding on all concerned. It is expected as the fruit of discussion. Of course, this conciliar unity depends on the presence of the Holy Spirit, and this is what distinguishes the Christian 'Council' from the workers' 'Soviets' of the Paris Commune. All the participants share this hope in the coming triumph of the truth. They all take it for granted that the consensus they are seeking may perhaps be greater, will indeed be greater, than the sum of their individual opinions or any compromise between rival positions or the complete triumph of the strongest faction or the strongest arguments. In Christian councils, at any rate in theory, individuals, groups, communities, churches come together and acknowledge one another as concrete forms of Christ's presence, as manifestations of the renewing power of the Holy Spirit. Precisely for this reason, they expect the result of their encounter to be a fuller appreciation of the larger truth. This is why they can afford to forego the code and count on a consensus, a consensus which will always be open-ended towards the future.

This model has many advantages. Unity is thought of as the growth of a diverse plurality towards deeper unity. It is essentially a pluralist unity. All participants in the council have equal rights and equal independence. But because these several independencies have to be seen as concrete forms of one and the same grace, instead of being obstacles to unity they become sources of unity. Apart from these independencies, the unity expected would simply not exist. *Any* unity which was less than the richness of these independencies would not simply be less than unity but actually the opposite of unity, namely, division, the dispersal of the multi-coloured grace of God (1 Pet. 4:10). The Christian conciliar model, in theory at least, is beyond the reach of such catch-questions as the relation between unity and diversity. Diversity is not fragmented unity. Unity is not cemented diversity. Unity is only conceivable and intelligible

as the mutual interaction of the many. All else is spurious
unity, artificial unity, the unity of Babel. And diversity can
only be thought of as the unity of the spectrum in all its
fullness, i.e. the unity of the one 'varied' grace of God to
each and every one. All else would not be diversity but
particularism, separatism, false individualism, the individuality of Cain.

All the other problems deriving from this basic problem are
then seen to be spurious problems. How reconcile the local
and the universal? Which comes first? The questions are
meaningless. For the universality which makes the Church
catholic is the universality of God's love towards human life in
all its concreteness, which is always local life; it is the
universality of the Spirit who fills, quickens and renews the
local. Thus the plurality of the local is the very structure of the
universal itself. The same applies to the question of continuity
and change. If, for the sake of the future triumph of the truth,
the consensus must be left open-ended and provisional, the
condition of continuity is change in response to the Spirit, and
the *continuum* of the Spirit's presence is the very root and
meaning of change.

It can be expressed in the following way: Conciliarity, the
Christian conciliar model, is the applied, actualized doctrine
of the Trinity. We are not to misinterpret this as just a smooth
formula making the best of a bad job. The immanent idea of
the Trinity reflects and safeguards the economic Trinity.
Among other things, it is a question of being able to
understand and hold firm to the conflict in God — of which
the cross is the most mysterious sign — as a genuine conflict
and not as shadow-boxing, not as a cosmic play-acting on the
part of God. The conciliar unity of the Church, in full
consensus with this, is therefore anything but a conflictless
unity. It is a struggle for the truth, waged in the common hope
of the coming victory of the truth. Not even unity and conflict
are to be divided, therefore. The open consensus of the council
is, in fact, conflict become constructive, productive of the
truth. And conflict is, in fact, the consensus in process of being
applied in the diverse situations and in response to the diverse
challenges. A consensus which failed to produce this conflict
and therefore to compel the continuation of the struggle for
truth, would not be the open-ended consensus of Christians.

Here and in the whole series of syntheses proposed here, there is, of course, a real danger of underestimating evil and sin. Both unity and diversity are always in danger of abnormal one-sided growths. Consensus *and* conflict can become barren, rigid and destructive. But Christian councils are — at least in theory — always councils under the cross of Jesus of Nazareth. The deadly power of evil *and* its dethronement are always already presupposed. In principle at least, therefore, the danger of underestimating what can happen in the struggle for truth is already taken care of.

Fully to appreciate the appeal of the conciliar model, one further point needs to be considered: namely, the fact that the open-ended consensus always remains subject to the test of approval or rejection by those at the local level. Christian councils have no mandate to issue commands. They work in the full knowledge that anything they produce must be acceptable to the majority. The veracity of a council is decided only in the history of its reception. The history of the reception of the Council of Chalcedon (which was considered at Louvain) is still not over even today, and the question of the reception of other councils, too, has been reopened by the ecumenical movement. To call the conciliar model 'basic democracy' is not just playing with words. Democracy subject to the presence of the Holy Spirit — that has always been the logic of the conciliar model.

Not that all this was made explicit in the document on conciliarity which was discussed at Louvain, not even in the summary fashion I have attempted here. But it was implicit in the document.

It was an eminently practical document. Its aim was:

1. To contribute to the understanding of what the ecumenical movement and the World Council of Churches really are. For here we see conciliarity in action. 'The ecumenical movement has both challenged and helped us to seek appropriate conciliar forms for our own time. Facing the question of the contemporary world, and drawn together by a common desire to serve the Lord together in the whole life and mission of the Church, the churches have been led in our own time to develop new forms of conciliarity — both within each church and in councils of churches at the local, national, regional and world levels. It is important that we should

reflect upon this fact, should endeavour to relate it to the
conciliar experience of the Church in the past, and should
seek more adequate forms of conciliarity for our day' (*Louvain*,
p. 226). ·

Another very important point here is that the *new* model of
unity is, at the same time, the oldest model, going back to the
first generations of Christians. *If* the ecumenical movement
and the World Council of Churches are conciliarity in action,
then an advance *beyond* the Toronto position is implied. The
ecclesiological character of the World Council of Churches is
affirmed, expressed in a formula. Both the nightmare of a
'Super Church' and the danger of any triumphalistic equation
of the existing instrument of international cooperation with
the conciliar unity of the Church are banished. The World
Council is an anticipation, a rough draft of the fullness of
conciliarity which is sought.

2. The 'ecclesiological formula' for interpreting the
ecumenical movement and the World Council of Churches is
extraordinarily flexible. It enables us to see at once the unity
of the whole gamut of motives and aims appealing to the
slogan of 'renewal'. All this rich diversity is part of the
inescapable search for the truth, a search still in mid-stream
and constantly being renewed because it is essential to find a
new form of open-ended consensus in the fundamentally new
situation of Christendom in today's world. Even the basically
incompatible concepts of renewal sponsored by the
administrators and the experimenters, the pragmatists and
the dreamers, the preservationists and the innovators, those
concerned with the *status quo* and those with their eyes on the
future, or, in more specific terms, the incompatible
standpoints of, for example, the Council of the Evangelical
Church in Germany and of the radical 'political prayer' group
in the Federal Republic, even these are here set in relationship
to each other *and* revitalized in a constructive way.

3. The aim of the document was also to differentiate clearly
between the goal to which the conciliar process in the
ecumenical movement is leading, on the one hand, and the
contemporary form of this process, on the other, yet at the
same time, just as clearly and convincingly, to link the two
together. 'The councils which have been created as
expressions of the ecumenical movement in our time do not

possess the fullness of conciliarity as it is to be seen in the great Councils of the early Church. . . . The central fact in true conciliarity is the active presence and work of the Holy Spirit. . . . But the acceptance of a Council as a true Council in the full sense of the word implies that its decisions are accepted by the Church as fully authoritative, and that it has been marked by or has led to full eucharistic fellowship' (*Louvain*, p. 227).

The presence of the Spirit, eucharistic fellowship, and full reception are therefore the marks of the 'genuinely universal council' to which the ecumenical movement must lead. Although we are still a great way off, we are coming noticeably nearer. Above all, the only way to prove whether or not the ecumenical movement *is* a conciliar event in this sense is for all of us to take it and try it out as such. In other words, if this conciliar formula *is* the right one, it means 'deepening our mutual commitment at all levels' (*ibid.* p. 226). Conciliarity is not just a game any more than Christian faith is a game. Nor can we just theorize about conciliarity. Only by practising conciliarity — which by its very nature only succeeds when it is taken seriously and not just 'on approval' — can we discover if it will culminate in the 'genuinely universal council'.

4. This means that, in the last analysis, the conciliar formula is primarily a directive for praxis. What is the next step? The document offers a fairly concrete description of the next step. It follows from the serious application of the criterion of 'deepening our mutual commitment at all levels'. It means making the ecumenical movement a basic dimension in the local communities, strengthening efforts for organic union and full eucharistic fellowship between the member churches, recognizing experimental ecumenism at the ground level, opening up the ecumenical movement for a thorough discussion and 'staging' of the conflicts which really tear Christendom apart, focussing ecumenical praxis on specific conflicts, cancelling the anathemas pronounced in the past, initiating an effort to achieve a common positive witness to the common faith (see below!).

In many respects this document is a brilliant achievement, the signal for a forward movement. Yet it fails to eliminate the ambivalence of motives and aims to which reference was made earlier.

Not the least appeal of this model lies in the way it permits
both a maximal and a minimal interpretation. Conciliarity,
whatever else it may mean, certainly means fully respecting
the independence and autonomy of all the participant groups,
communities and churches. The conciliar model banishes the
danger of a 'Super Church' and the danger of overtaxing the
readiness of the member churches for compromise. But this
could easily be simply a soft-option to allow the member
churches to extricate themselves from the pressure inevitably
exerted on them by the existence of the ecumenical
movement. We must stick uncompromisingly to our own
identity and integrity, they could say, precisely *for the sake of*
this goal of a 'genuinely universal council'. Everything else,
every specific advance, is subject to the proviso of the presence
of the Holy Spirit as well as to the proviso that reception by
the Christian communities remains completely open. All
could remain as before, therefore, and even take a step
backwards and yet leave the churches with the com-
fortable feeling that, even so, they were still on the
'ecumenical pathway' pointed out by the new formula! On
this interpretation, the conciliar model represents a Gamaliel
strategy: wait and see if this be of God!

The maximal interpretation is no less dangerous. Pushed
too far, the conflict-oriented strategy of the formula
legitimizes every confrontation, every trial of strength, every
'civil war' in the churches, every bible-thumping guerilla. The
formula's fondness for concretizing the universal in the
particular encourages the neurotic preoccupation of every
minority, every brand of separatism, with its own image. And
the truth that only by taking conciliar praxis seriously can we
learn whether or not it produces reunion can also give *carte
blanche* to impatient ecumenists. The document itself provided
a prod of this kind — though in question form, of course, since
it was an ecumenical document! — 'What are the
preconditions for a true Council? Could there be a "reunion"
Council which did not presuppose eucharistic fellowship and
full consensus, but met seeking and expecting these as gifts of
the Holy Spirit?' (*Louvain*, p. 227). What was to stop anyone
thinking of the then forthcoming Fifth Assembly of the World
Council of Churches in 1975 as just an 'all or nothing' test

case and dismissing all caution on the part of the institutions as ecumenical pusillanimity or even as a refusal to 'deepen our common commitment'?

The conciliarity model was and is a very promising one. Yet it does not alter the fact that the aims of the ecumenical movement are unresolved. That indecision cannot be eliminated by ecumenical *documents* at all.

This becomes even clearer when we turn our attention to the other element of 'visible unity' mentioned in the new constitution of the World Council of Churches: viz. the *one* faith!

In his report on Faith and Order work in the years immediately preceding Louvain, Lukas Vischer, staff director of the Faith and Order Secretariat in Geneva, took the bull by the horns (*Louvain*, p. 200 ff.). The burden of his whole report was that the time for action had come. But, in the last analysis, this meant that the moment had come for the churches to tackle their most difficult task: namely, work on a new ecumenical confession of faith, the preparatory work for a binding conciliar act of confession. Not even Lukas Vischer quite dared to spell that out in such precise terms, but the logic of his exposition was quite clear.

We had spent so much time reflecting on what *no longer* divides us today and why it no longer divides us. We were pretty well agreed on this. Then we had given more and more attention to the fact that in the midst of the storms of our time we were all more or less *in the same boat*. Internal and external forces were driving us more and more closely together. Now at last the time had come for us to say what *positively* we had in common, what we all believe, what we all confess, what we all preach. 'Has the time not come for the Commission to turn more resolutely to the task of clarifying the fundamental affirmation of the Christian faith? To ask the question: How do we together fulfil our calling today "to account for the hope that is in us"? To try to formulate together the faith in Christ which binds us together? To be concerned more or less exclusively with the nature and structures of the Church is in the long run inadequate and unsatisfactory. The churches are passing through a time of challenging experiences and in the years to come they are likely to undergo very great changes. Such a time brings with it the danger of self-preoccupation,

not so much the preoccupation of Narcissus, who fell in love
with himself, but more the self-preoccupation of a sick man
who is concerned with the changes taking place in his own
body and determines his expectations accordingly. The
Commission on Faith and Order faces the same temptation.
Its necessary and inevitable concern with the theme of unity
leads it too easily to an unhealthy concentration on
ecclesiology. Is it not essential for the Commission, therefore,
to try to show how we can together express the hope of the
Gospel? Must we not try to formulate together the centre from
which we begin, the source by which we live? The Church's
identity is inseparable from this hope, and it is only
recognizable when it knows how to speak of this hope. . . .
The question of truth in the Church needs clarification' (*Louvain*, p.
209 f.).

The Commission in Louvain reacted somewhat coolly to
this challenge, despite all the qualifications and reservations
in which it was wrapped. They did not simply reject it. The
justice, good sense and urgency of the signal was too obvious
for that. The theme 'Common Expression of Faith' (giving
account of the hope that is in us) appeared, therefore, at the
head of the list of studies to be undertaken after Louvain. But
the preparatory document in which the proposal had been
presented was three times revised in plenary alone and what
finally remained of it in the conspectus of future studies had
lost its sharp edges and was mainly formulated in terms of
what the study did *not* intend. It seemed to the Commission
that the time had certainly not yet arrived for so dangerous an
enterprise as confessing the faith together — not to mention a
common confession of faith!

It is easy to see from the discussion in plenary where the
stumbling block lay.

(*a*) Whereas in Vischer's report the Commission itself was
seen as the agency for this project, though with the full
participation of the ecumenical constituency, the formulation
as revised in plenary shifted the emphasis to the 'members of
the churches', to 'individual groups' in 'different situations'.
The Commission wanted its working group to initiate and
encourage this process, and the end-product which it
envisaged was to be 'something in the form of a declaration'
which the churches 'would be able to issue jointly'. In other

words, whereas Vischer had quite explicitly called for 'a common statement of our faith', what the Commission had in mind was an experimental process in different local contexts. This would still leave the Commission itself with the task of evaluating theoretically 'what had actually emerged in these different situations as the essence of the Gospel' and what were the 'criteria of identity' in the change in actual confession from place to place and from time to time. 'The study will have to consider in particular the following basic theological issues: the understanding of truth and the possibility of discerning a "hierarchy" of truths; the relationship between unity and diversity; between truth and communion; the respective place of individual confession and confession by the community; of doctrine, proclamation and prayer' (*Louvain*, p. 240). Even if it is impossible to put one's finger on the precise difference, Vischer had obviously meant something different. But the Commission 'referred his proposal to the committees' and turned the experiment in confessing together into a Faith and Order study on 'the confession of faith today'. Even that was not to be despised, but it was clearly less than what was asked for.

(*b*) There was one very striking passage in the text as initially presented in plenary session: 'The question as to the audience to which such a common declaration would be addressed seems not to make any decisive difference to its content. *It is impossible for us to undertake to differentiate clearly between members of the Church and those who do not belong to it, if for no other reason than that even Christians themselves are again and again assailed by doubts*. When members of the Church seek to grasp more firmly what they really believe, they can only do so as they also constantly have present to their minds the questions of their contemporaries.' Discussion in plenary became particularly heated at this point. To blur the boundaries of the Church in this way and to compare the temptations of Christians to the unbelief of the despairing was obviously to saddle everyone with the embattled feelings of the disintegrating Central European territorial churches. In the socialist world, the post-revolutionary world, and in the Third World, where Christendom is only a tiny dispersed minority in the midst of millions of non-Christians, the despairing attitude of a piety 'after the death of God', as expressed here,

was quite meaningless. And this illustrates the ambiguity of
the entire proposal. All of us can say: Yes, there's a crisis. Yes,
it's time for a new confession. But each of us means something
quite different in each situation. Some are thinking of an up-
to-date statement of what has always been confessed, since
the pressure of unbelief comes to them mainly from the
outside. Others are thinking of the erosion of faith from
within, the process of secularization and pluralization among
their church members. These are looking for a new certainty
when they identify themselves unconditionally with the
despairing at the point of their despair. In fact, these are two
fundamentally different positions, even if many shades of
distinction need to be allowed for. The attempt to deal with
both needs together seems to distort them both, to minimize
the pressures from without and to underestimate the erosion
from within. The formulation adopted by the plenary simply
omitted the sentence we have italicized.

(*c*) The same tendency is also met at another explosive
point. Here, even the penultimate version still asked certain
groups to investigate 'how exactly specific themes of the
Gospel which are the object of special controversy today (for
example, Christ's resurrection and second coming, the
kingdom of God) are to be understood and made intelligible
today'. In other words, even the central affirmations of the
Christian faith are being challenged today. But the majority
of the churches are still not ready to admit that. More
precisely, they are not prepared to make that the starting
point for a 'coherent account of Christian hope'. The words in
brackets were simply' omitted from the final version. The
problem in the minds of those who produced the original
version was not thereby exorcised, of course. Consideration of
the ambiguity was simply postponed.

That throws the difficulty of Lukas Vischer's challenge into
even sharper relief. Critical theology had hitherto been
employed in Faith and Order on the demolition or
relativization of differences. It was ideally suited for such a
task. Vischer now wanted the positive test: What new
certainty emerges out of this process of clarification? He
wanted the clearance work to end and the construction work
to begin, or at least work on the plans. But this called for
agreement on what building materials were available and how

they fitted together: in other words, it meant tackling an ecumenical christology, an ecumenical soteriology, work on the doctrine of the Trinity. The underlying foundations of the negative consensus needed to be investigated. Finally, it meant getting down to the discussion of the substance of the different ecclesiologies. And all this against a background of growing pluralism which makes people afraid of real doctrinal discussions even within the confessions, even within the territorial churches, even among the clergy and the theologians in the most disciplined church districts; within a situation in which all the churches were more and more tempted to 'rule out' dissensus on central questions and to postpone clarifications. In Vischer's view precisely this general state of uncertainty was the right moment for Christians to put the question of truth and to do so as a matter of necessity. But dared one do that? The majority in Louvain decided: No!

So far as the question of 'one eucharistic fellowship' was concerned, we at least had a promising formula, even if it was differently interpreted, the concept of 'conciliarity'. All we had, basically, in the question of the 'one faith' was a decision that the time was not yet ripe. That did not rule out study and cooperation. But the hesitancy about aims is well-documented.

2. Indecision about Methods

The capacity of the ecumenical movement to act is vested almost exclusively in the member churches and their official organs. But the member churches are in two minds. What their representatives say and promise at ecumenical meetings, while certainly not just forgotten when they return home, is still essentially their private opinion. There is no certainty that ecumenical findings, decisions, recommendations and problems will ever reach the official agencies of the member churches, unless it concerns finance. William Temple's dictum still holds good: the only authority the World Council has is 'the weight it carries in the member churches by its intrinsic wisdom'.

The Council and its agencies have very limited means of ensuring that this weight — which has grown considerably since Temple's time — is brought to bear in the member churches.

(a) Consultation

Visser 't Hooft tells how, when he was called by John R.
Mott to Geneva to become Youth Secretary, he sat for a while
in his office not rightly knowing how to begin his work.
Finally he went to Mott and asked him what he should do.
Mott simply growled: 'If I'd known that, I wouldn't have
needed to bring you here!' Visser 't Hooft tells us he went
back to his office and decided to call a consultation![29]

Consultation is the chief method in ecumenical work,
ecumenical activity. Individual achievements, inspirations,
ideas and plans are all of them important but it is only
through consultation that they acquire ecumenical status
and influence. They have to pass through the filter of
an interconfessional, international, intercultural, interdisciplinary, consultative process. In this process they are
changed; quite different viewpoints, insights and concerns are
absorbed and transform them, or else make them into so
much waste paper. The consensus which is developed in this
process is frequently far duller than the inspiration by which
it lives. But it represents a common awareness of the problem.
It represents authority for action, within the limits of action
possible for ecumenical agencies. It also represents the start
and the instrument of an opinion-forming process which at its
best could ultimately reach whole churches.

By and large, the main working departments of the World
Council of Churches — World Mission and Evangelism,
Faith and Order, the Commission of the Churches for
International Affairs, Church and Society, and so on — are
consultations on a permanent basis, advisory bodies for the
purpose of mutual counsel. The conciliarity model which the
World Council propagates is *de facto* its own well-tried *modus
operandi*, its own way of working.

Essential as this method is, however, it is also in many
respects indecisive and this indecisiveness is growing.

Its main strength is also its main weakness. It rests on the
force of argument. Meanwhile, however, that arguments do
not change structures has become a commonplace. And in the
case of the churches, it is the ecumenical consultations
themselves which have produced this result. Structures
represent needs, interests, historical experience, public
opinion. They only change when the interests and the public

opinion reflected in them change, and even then only by organized pressure. For existing structures have their own inherent weight. They have the character of law. They are kept going by an administrative machine and this machine seeks to perpetuate itself. The general fear of the insecurity a change in structures would bring with it is itself sufficient to protect even the most obsolete structures for quite a time. From the standpoint of social psychology, the truth is that even an unsatisfactory behavioural pattern is better than no pattern at all. Only when a new alternative pattern appears, as a result of organizing the difference between existing structures and the changed interests, does structural change have any prospect of success.

But structural change, in the broadest sense, is precisely what the goal of 'visible unity' implies. To achieve this, therefore, a change in public opinion in the churches is absolutely essential. To achieve this opinion, the method of consultation is not enough. It does, of course, change the opinion of those directly involved, and, *if* they are good communicators and have mastered the technique of systematic opinion shaping, also the people to whom they are related.

But it is just here that palpable weaknesses are revealed in the ecumenical method of consultation. For example, even today we still have no methodology or didactics of ecumenical consultation; no analysis whatever of more than fifty years' experience and not even the ghost of an awareness that a problem even *exists* here. Ecumenical consultation continues as before to be a quite naïve, quite unmonitored and unmonitorable 'round table' discussion. No one knows quite what is going on in terms of group dynamics; no one knows which are the factors which make for success and which militate against it, or render it impossible. No one knows the sort of preparation that is needed if all the participants are to enter fully into the consultation and make their maximum contribution to it. No one knows the anxiety levels involved in an intercultural, international, interconfessional discussion. No one has a clear picture of the hierarchy of prejudices introduced into it, the interests at stake which may have little or nothing whatever to do with its theme, the surd elements which have to be reckoned with. No one knows the basic principles of responsible leadership of group discussion in such complex group situations. No one knows the minimum requirements of follow-up work, evaluation, recording, publication, or feedback, if even a successful consultation is not subsequently to run into disaster. It is almost as if communication and learning theory, group psychology and scientific educational methods had simply never existed for the ecumenical movement. Consultations are an exercise yard for charismatics and the only plausible explanation one can offer for the improbable success of the ecumenical movement is that it has particular attractions for charismatics. The good and evil spirits that are sure to be present in such a difficult group situation are simply let loose in the hope that the Holy Spirit will also turn up.

When one remembers that only superficially is an ecumenical consultation a discussion between equal partners with equal rights, and that by opting in favour of just *one* of the world languages (English), in favour of just *one* procedural method (the Anglo-Saxon parliamentary procedure) and just *one* style of discussion (the Oxbridge style), far-reaching decisions have already been made determining what contributions and findings are and are not possible — then this absence of verification becomes all the more mysterious. There must be some method behind it.

The theory of sinister manipulations must be discarded! The explanation is simply the well-known formula: 'Leave well alone!' To discuss this dynamic of ecumenical consultations, in fact, would mean tackling the much-invoked 'non-theological factors' but now no longer at a safe distance as historical factors which have played and still play a part in the divisions of the Church; now they would have to be discussed as factors we can actually see in operation now. And initially at least, this would be a very painful business. Above all, what would happen to the spirit of conciliarity if it had to face the fact that struggles over status and pecking order also play a part even in ecumenical conferences, that even here there are 'first' and 'last', and that these social and psychological factors combine with differences of language, culture, life styles, thought patterns, conflicting interests in world politics, in such a way that what actually happens at the level of conscious argument is highly questionable and therefore deserving of investigation?

The irresolution of the ecumenical movement generally can largely be explained by its strange refusal right down to the present to take really seriously its early insight into the importance of these non-theological factors. This itself has only served to increase the force of that insight. At first it was regarded more as a marginal irritant, the symptom of a residual worldliness in the life of the Church. Painful though it was, it simply had to be borne with. Then it began to be realized that these socio-cultural and psychological factors were also operative even in the development of doctrine and church order, and that the logic of incarnation and the indigenization of the Church meant that Christian truth was necessarily subject to this all-pervasive reality. It meant that even the most central utterances of faith (the titles we give to Jesus, for example) are conditioned and permeated by it. Finally, too, the fact had to be faced — in the main theme of Louvain, for example — that these 'non-theological' factors are not only the medium of church doctrine but also influence the churches very directly in the shape of the conflict potential of world politics. Today it is these factors which are the really divisive ones in the churches and between the churches, whereas the old interconfessional conflicts have for a long time been on the reserve list.

Yet there is great reluctance to draw the only possible conclusion from this insight: namely, that ecumenical theology, indeed theology of any kind, not only needs interdisciplinary assistance but *is itself becoming more and more an interdisciplinary exercise*. Like anthropology, theology, too, has to become a joint undertaking of all the sciences — human, social and historical. If theology is concerned with the truth about reality, then all man's knowledge and experience of reality must be brought into the reflection process and exposed to the test of truth. There are, of course, many sorts of data and even all-important criteria which only competent specialists can contribute here: biblical philologists, historians specializing in church history, experts in the history of philosophy and theology, experts in the sociology of the churches and the psychology of religion. There will also be those whose special field of knowledge is a particular social praxis, that of the Church, which has special need for theological reflection on its mandate and role. But these people are not 'theologians' in some superior sense, compared with other specialists and practicians involved in the reflective process. Theology is not so much a profession as the common theme of all professions. That was what theology was when the *universitas litterarum* came into existence and, by a complicated route, that is what it has once more become.

But this means that the range of competence and working methods in ecumenical consultations is far too limited. It becomes impossible to leave the 'other disciplines' to formulate the questions and theology to provide the answers, or vice versa. All have to join both in formulating the questions and in trying to find the answers. From a methodological standpoint, of course, this is rather like trying to 'square the circle' and would have incalculable consequences for the way the ecumenical movement organizes the consultation process. But for the moment, this approach has yet to be accepted ecumenically. For the moment, it is still the view that ecumenical work is chiefly the concern of professional theologians (even though they themselves find it increasingly difficult to distinguish their own subject, methods, style of thinking, and so on, from those of other disciplines). The others are only there to fetch and carry. A parochial theology may still find it possible to accept this division of labour. But an ecumenical theology with a definite programme in view, namely, the reunion of Christendom, pays the price for accepting it, namely, by continuing to be inconclusive, hesitant, irresolute.

We have still to mention the fact that even the scientific equipment of the ecumenical consultation process is so modest that it would be an exaggeration even to call it spartan. Even a cosmetics factory today cannot manage without an elaborate research department. The most improbable problems today are deemed worthy of their special research teams and promotion campaigns. Yet the ecumenical movement, in business for the future of a religious community with a membership running into billions, still has no research institute of its own, not even a theological one, let alone an interdisciplinary one, still has no 'Institute for Advanced Ecumenical Studies'. The theory of ecumenical praxis is essentially a leisure time hobby.

(b) Publication

Whole libraries of books have been written during the fifty years of the ecumenical movement's existence. Neither at the world level nor in the member churches has there been any lack of industry in publishing. Yet it is only in very recent days that professional publishers have appeared on the ecumenical scene who have learned the business of preparing and disseminating ecumenical news and ideas and brought it to a certain pitch of professional expertise.

Here again we find — a classic case of self-contradiction — the enormous influence of an almost superstitious trust in the power of argument characteristic of Christians with their understandable tendency to identify the Word of God with the words of men. It has hardly dawned on us that, as the product of an involved process of consensus building, ecumenical words are almost like a secret code for all ordinary readers, even more difficult for them to understand than the already very esoteric language used by the member churches.

We have learned something, at least, from the controversies over the Programme to Combat Racism. Ecumenical words only acquire 'news value' when the interests of church and society are damaged or even merely threatened by ecumenical action. Then the mass media step in and simplify ecumenical language by putting it into a relevant and plausible secular context. What is published, of course, is inevitably rather painful for the devotees of the ecumenical movement. But without this 'alienation' there would never be any communication or controversy worthy the name, not even in the case of the most explosive themes. The internal ecumenical press is rather like a circular letter, only reaching the already converted. Even its circulation figures are quite derisory. Every weekly church paper has a far larger circulation.

It is only recently that any serious thought has been given to the conditions in which ecumenical communication is possible. And yet we talk at the same time about conciliarity and its acid test in the universal reception of ecumenical findings by the local communities! But how shall the local communities accept that of which they have not yet even heard? Not to mention the deep-seated resistance of parochially-minded people to take in anything which comes to them from some different quarter of the landscape.

(c) Visitation

Visitation, travel, is not only the most ancient method of establishing contacts and communication, a *mutuum colloquum fratrum,* mutual concern and responsibility, it is also the most modern. Ecumenical officials travel far more than commercial travellers. Above all, they travel further and on far more difficult business. They cannot count on their 'wares' supplying some existing consumers' 'demand'. On the contrary, what they have to offer meets with considerable competition with local needs and interests in different places. An ecumenical travelling salesman of American origin comes as a dangerous stranger when he visits his own country. It is always money he is after. He wants to persuade bureaucrats, who inevitably live and think from one budget to the next, to commit themselves to long-term plans and programmes. He wants to pry into the cellars and attics of the member churches where everything is untidy. He wants to develop ecumenical awareness among the church members and thus to incite public opinion in the churches against the parochial structures.

I'm exaggerating, of course. It is certainly not true that the official structures of the member churches are particularly lacking in ecumenical awareness. There is indeed a considerable ecumenical potential to be found among church administrators. Among them especially, indeed, for it is mainly here that we find the people who participate in ecumenical consultations. But these opposite numbers of the ecumenical visitors find themselves in a permanent state of confusion as to their role, and this precisely because of the ecumenical movement. For the ecumenical movement is a fundamental challenge to all territorial churchmanship. It came into existence, in fact, precisely because the territorial churches could no longer evade the fact that world developments increasingly called them in question. They objectified and institutionalized this sense of crisis in the World Council of Churches. But this means that ecumenical visits inevitably remind them of this crisis. Ecumenical visits are a signal to strike camp! At the same time, however, the church administrations also embody and represent the needs and interests of their constituencies. And, particularly in this period of crisis, these needs and interests tend to be predominantly conservative and defensive.

Another factor, of course, is the nature of ecclesial life and participation. Public opinion as it comes to expression among church people is in fact the opinion of the active among them, the ones who attend services and participate fully in the congregational programmes. In the main, these are not the people who have the new contemporary outlook or share that sense of a vast all-embracing transformation to which the ecumenical movement is a response. Or, if they do have it, it makes them anxious and the intensity of their church life may be the expression of this anxiety. But if this is the section of public opinion in the churches which church administrators represent, they tend to be anti-ecumenical. On their first stops on their ecumenical journeys, ecumenical visitors seldom find any clear sense of unanimity, at any rate.

There is also a basic rule for ecumenical visitors, one which corresponds to the World Council's view of itself as an instrument in the service of the member churches. Ecumenical visits must begin with the church officials and with the national or local Christian councils. That is where the programme must be drawn up. That is where the choice is made as to the people one sees, or does not see. That is where the visitor is briefed about particular situations of conflict and given appropriate advice. Visits which bypass this process are not wanted, and would in any case only be possible for a visitor who knows the local situation intimately.

The inevitable result is a fatal curtailment of possible contacts and impressions. For a visitor to find his way into the ecumenical underground where extremely interesting things are happening is almost impossible because relations between this underground and the official church are tense, to put it mildly. It is also difficult for him to enter the no-man's-land of congregations as yet untouched by the ecumenical movement. And the extent to which a visitor is able to gain first-hand knowledge of the church's environment depends entirely on how much importance those who arrange the programme attach to this aspect of a visit.

Once again, I am guilty of an intolerable over-simplification. Ecumenical visits by invitation do indeed happen. Invitations are also received from the underground and from the areas around the churches. It is still true that, within the member churches, the ecumenical movement bears all the marks of an 'in-group' of devotees. When it is a matter of arranging journeys, questions of possible contacts, the selection of people for committees, the same names crop up time after time. On paper, the ecumenical movement represents millions of people. Its life depends on the cooperation of a few thousand. And basically the problem is one of inherently contradictory structures. Even the method of visitation is indecisive.

(d) Demonstration

The most effective propaganda — in the churches and outside — is action, praxis. To say that is not to play off action against speech or reflection. But discussion and reflection are all the more productive and decisive, they engender a greater readiness and capacity to learn, the more they are focussed on a definite and tangible praxis.

But the ecumenical movement is at its most practical in the fields of *diakonia* and development service. It finds no difficulty in carrying conviction there. But it is not so easy to translate the central theme of the ecumenical movement — the reunion of Christians — into praxis. The practical experiments of grass-roots ecumenism are in bad odour because they betray over-impatience and too little respect for the official protocol of interchurch relations. There is, of course, the praxis *at* the consultations themselves, but this is of direct evidential value only to the participants.

Important exceptions can be mentioned: Weeks of Prayer, work camps, campaigns conducted by national or local Christian councils or committees, such as the annual Whitsuntide ecumenical gatherings in Augsburg in Germany. Even local activities in support of ecumenical service and Christian Aid programmes are more than fund-raising efforts and represent a considerable educational enterprise reaching even people outside the churches.

Yet here too there is a radical inconclusiveness. The ecumenical movement's problem of 'theory and practice' is also a structural one. The only way of testing the sturdiness of the ecumenical bridge formulas would be to conduct a controlled experiment which would itself set in train a reflection process fed by experience and constantly feeding back into praxis. The churches, however, are largely inhibited from initiating such experiments because each experiment would create a precedent. Moreover, the seat of religious truth is the conscience. Can one experiment with consciences? Can one experiment with living people and their relationships — and a congregation is surely a complex of such relationships? To talk of church 'experiments', we have now come to realize, is an extremely ambiguous use of language. Human relations and processes of human development are always 'for real'. They are irreversible. The experimental conditions cannot be varied. The findings cannot be transferred. We now understand why churches hesitate to permit practical experiments and why they distrust them, especially since they are mostly associated with anarchistic ground-level ecumenism. Such praxis is not just a dress-rehearsal for the real performance, it *is* the performance. And, the churches think, we are not yet sure enough for that.

But this is a vicious circle. A theory without the corresponding praxis is hollow, and the more elaborate it becomes, the falser, the more illusory it becomes. Praxis without corresponding theory — even the anarchistic praxis based on the deliberate theory of not waiting for majorities — is blind. The longer it goes on, the more schismatic it becomes. According to the constitution of the ecumenical movement, the only praxis which could authenticate or disqualify its findings would be the praxis of the member churches themselves. But if the churches had been ripe for this praxis on a broad front, the ecumenical movement in its present form would by now be out of date. There appears to be only one way out of this impasse: real serious confrontation with ecumenism at the ground level. But, once again, that, too, would already, in itself, be the ecumenical change!

(e) Leadership Training

From the very beginning, the ecumenical movement has been concerned to recruit and train leaders. But its resources for doing this are very limited. Establishments such as the Bossey Ecumenical Institute are accessible to very few and the participation of people from the Third World is becoming so

expensive as to reduce even these possibilities still more
drastically. There are training centres in the regions and in
the member churches, too, of course. But an ecumenical rule
of thumb insists that, in order to be able to work with the
different Christianities and to develop ecumenical awareness,
people need first-hand experience of world-dimension and the
complete universal range of these different forms of Christian
obedience. A territorially contracted leadership training also
produces a territorially lopsided ecumenicity.

University and post-graduate courses for church workers
do, of course, include ecumenical studies, but these still tend
to be peripheral concerns. It seems highly unlikely that such
training could make ecumenical thought and action an
integral dimension of church thought and action. No real
broadening of limited horizons takes place.

The most effective ecumenical training, the most successful
school of ecumenical leadership, is still that provided by
actual participation in the ecumenical process, in meetings
and consultations, in study conferences and ecumenical
service programmes. The only real ecumenical training is 'in
service' training. But again, the number of those who have
this privilege is small. When one remembers that the aim is to
produce a qualitative change in public opinion in the
churches, even the ecumenical scholarship programme and
the ecumenical use of exchanges between students and
migrant-workers, which are developing into an avalanche in
this interdependent world, have so far produced far too little.

There is one other special problem here. At one time, the
World Student Christian Federation, the world YMCA and
YWCA organizations, and other international youth and
student associations were important training grounds for
ecumenical leadership in the World Council of Churches. So
far, thank God, they have escaped complete integration into
the ecumenical movement of the *churches*. Incidentally, it is
very hard to know whether the integration of the three main
streams (International Missionary Council, Faith and Order
movement, Life and Work movement) in the ecumenical
movement of the churches was not perhaps achieved much too
soon, and whether the result was not perhaps to turn a
productive conflict into an unproductive one which severely
restricts the Council's power of action. At any rate, the real

leadership trainers remained outside. This means, however, that they are still suspected of 'non-denominationalism', as it used to be called in the early days. In other words, they are suspected of lacking a due sense of responsibility to church and confession. The turbulent pluralism which has overtaken theologies and attitudes has hit these movements much more severely than even the churches and the World Council itself. The result has been deeper mistrust on the part of the member churches. What these movements produce in the way of ecumenical resources tends more and more to find its way, therefore, into the anarchist underground of ground-level ecumenism.

This method, therefore, suffers from the same sort of inconclusiveness that we have found in other fields. To educate and train ecumenical 'multipliers' of sufficient quality and in sufficient numbers to produce the needed 'forward leap' in public opinion in the member churches, would itself presuppose that 'forward leap'! One essential presupposition would be a radical change in the religious and moral education of infants and a transformation in the contents and methods of church instruction from the primary department upward. A sense of universality, the capacity to act with a sense of responsibility towards the whole world, is rooted in a liberation of the conscience from its parochial imprisonment. And this imprisonment begins at a very early stage.

(f) The Ecumenical Infrastructure

The World Council of Churches is simply the world level of a movement which is organized at many levels. There are the regional ecumenical organizations. In almost every country there are national Christian Councils or similar bodies. There is also a growing number of ecumenical agencies at district and parish level.

Yet this does not automatically mean a reinforcement of the ecumenical movement as one which seeks the world-wide reunion of Christendom. Christian Councils can only act to the extent that their member churches are prepared to act in concert. But it is precisely at the local level that the short-term interests of the churches often conflict, and only their long-term interests which coincide. In general, weak Christian Councils diminish the weight of the ecumenical movement as a whole, since they only complicate matters. As an institution, the World Council has to act through these agencies which often does not improve relations with the member churches. Strong Christian Councils, on the other hand, have a double-edged importance. In cases of conflict, their member churches tend to regard them as a kind of ecumenical Trojan horse; they appear to decide their own policies and to pursue their own interests. But to the extent that they take themselves seriously as really representing the regional ecumenical interests of their members, they strengthen the centrifugal forces in the ecumenical movement. It then becomes easy for them to come into conflict with Geneva.

Basically, an examination of the ecumenical movement's methods and forms of action confronts us with one and the same problem. The ecumenical movement understands itself as a movement of the *churches*, but the churches themselves are undecided as to how far they should go in their ecumenical commitment. This is why the ecumenical movement itself is inconclusive.

3.   What Real Support has the Ecumenical Movement at the Ground Level?

It has been amply demonstrated that the World Council of Churches is handicapped by the incompatibility of its two basic functions. On the one hand, it is an instrument for international cooperation between the churches; in this role it has to implement the concrete decisions of its members, nothing more. On the other hand, it is the *avant-garde* of reunited Christendom, an anticipation of coming union and renewal, a post-dated cheque; in this role it has to think, speak and act prophetically, to challenge the churches and to set them moving.

In both roles it acts on behalf of the churches. It did not anoint itself to the prophetic calling, as an *avant-garde*. The member churches want this disturbance out of the future. Through their representatives, they press for advance towards ecumenical consensus, progress in ecumenical action, and themselves contribute to these.

But this double role leads to a growing credibility gap. The difference between ecumenical promises and their redemption by the member churches, between verbal advances and continued parochialism in church praxis, grows apace.

Occasionally there is an explosion. If the World Council is not to forfeit all credibility, it has to take action itself. By doing so it puts pressure on the churches to move, and they are unequal to it. What then follows is a sort of 'moment of truth' for the ecumenical movement.

The most recent example was the conflict over the World Council's Programme to Combat Racism. It produced a series of reverberations. An analysis of what happened is overdue. It necessarily leads to a number of conclusions about the decisiveness and indecisiveness of the ecumenical movement.

Here I can highlight only one aspect of the conflict over the anti-racism programme. This conflict showed that the church membership for the most part is almost completely unconscious of the ecumenical dimension. What it knows about ecumenical progress would not take long to tell. To a large extent, it does not even want to know about it, because all of us tend instinctively to fade out any facts or ideas which call our cherished identity in question.

What happened in Germany? The public and the mass media seemed thunderstruck when it became known that the World Council of Churches had decided to give grants (for humanitarian purposes) from its Special Fund to organizations struggling against institutionalized racism in government, economics and society or organizing the victims of racism politically and, above all, in the special situation in South Africa, not to exclude even the use of violence. 'CHURCH MONEY FOR GUERILLAS?' was one of the milder headlines!

The active church membership was polarised — especially when one provincial Church set aside part of its income from church taxes for the Fund — along predictable lines. Christians who wanted a Church committed to law and order were up in arms, threatened to leave the Church, felt that everything they held dear was in danger. Those who were critical of Church and society and hoping for change, for the most part young people, breathed a sigh of relief. The church authorities, who had to consider the needs and interests of those who paid church taxes and respect the general opinion of the church members, overwhelmingly rejected the general direction in which the Programme to Combat Racism was moving. The unattached groups, who in any case believed that the Church should break with the *religion civile*, were solidly in favour.

But both sides in the conflict used the racism problem more as an excuse to pursue an already existing conflict. Neither side really seemed to understand the ecclesiological relevance of the problem of racism, the radical challenge which the revolt of the powerless presented to North Atlantic church life, even to its 'progressive' wing. Otherwise the discussion would not have been hurriedly diverted to the spurious alternative of violence or non-violence.

The reaction of the church authorities and synods was particularly instructive. It amounted to a 'Yes, but . . .'. At this level, everybody knew that this ecumenical 'forward leap' on the racism issue had years of preparation behind it. They were familiar with the statements. Leading representatives of this group had even helped to draft them. So long as this remained only on paper, it seemed to concern only far-off places. It was just the familiar church radicalism 'speaking to the situation', which seldom led to anything. But now it was actually dividing their own home base. At the same time, it showed an almost complete neglect of ecumenical education in the congregations. It showed that the ecumenical dimension had never really been assimilated, only tacked on. They were in the situation of a Church without a constituency, a pastor without a congregation. That was not what they had expected. They were against racism, but. . . .

For various reasons, Germany was in this respect an exception. A failure to come to terms with the past made the racism problem, like the problem of violence, in one way or another *tabu*. We cannot use what happened in Germany to draw general conclusions about the overall state of the ecumenical movement. Certainly ecumenism is not everywhere quite so 'base-less', quite so lacking in ground level support.

Yet it is true that all over the world, the awareness and conscience of ordinary church members, most of them at any rate, has not kept pace with the ecumenical movement.

This presents the ecumenical movement with a vital question: How is it to set in motion the learning process which is absolutely essential if the ecumenical possibility is to become the reality of Christendom? At present there is not only no adequate answer, there is no answer at all to this question. At least none which could provide a basis for praxis.

There is no ecumenical *didactic*, no theory and no method of how the world outlook with which alone the Church today can be the Church, a Christianity relevant to the present time, is to be acquired.

Above all, there is no ecumenical *social didactic*, no theory and no method for producing an atmosphere, a situation of tension, in church and society, in which individuals, groups, communities and church officials are really set free for a learning process which carries them beyond their previous level of information and awareness. Explosions like the conflict over the Programme to Combat Racism produce such a climate, such a state of tension. To some extent that has been demonstrated. But the distortions caused by a 'messy conflict' such as this, the frictional losses, are unnecessarily high. People should not be plunged into a state of alarm when this could easily be avoided by a better technique of social education.

As we have already seen from an analysis of the goals and practical methods of the ecumenical movement, responsibility for the inconclusiveness of the movement seems to lie principally with the member churches, i.e. with the church administrations, the decision-making bodies and the staff of the member churches. But that is by no means the whole story.

The failure to translate the new experience of Christendom into renewal at the ground level of the churches is not attributable to ill-will or negligence on the part of the bureaucrats or professional ecumenists in the member churches. Nor is it due to a shortage of information. The real trouble seems to lie, rather, in an insufficient liberty of conscience. The problem of how to produce new experiences can only be solved if we first make sure that people are really able to enter into and assimiliate experiences of this kind *conscientiously* instead of being automatically shut out from them by fear of losing their own identity and integrity.

The language of traditional piety had focussed on a person's immediate responsibilities and duties, on experiences of conflict and reconciliation in the primary groups of family and the neighbourhood, and on the immediately tangible relations of command and obedience in professional and public life. But the very dimensions of the huge modern city, the division of labour in industry, the political organization of the masses at the national level, these things are hard to translate properly into this traditional language of the conscience, which it has largely learned from religion. And even the primary experiences still have pre-industrial labels. Basically, these labels derive from the problems of the child from infancy to adolescence, not from those of the adult in society. In other words, the adult world, with its modern forms of organization and its conflicts, has never really been assimilated, never become articulate in the conscience. And since religion lives by its harmony with the conscience, we still have no better term than 'rule, dominion' to describe the liberating work of the crucified Christ and no better term than 'service' or 'obedience' for the response of the liberated person. The global experience and responsibility of the second half of the twentieth century cannot be expressed in this language, at least not deeply enough to touch the conscience, to liberate and reorient it. Christians are living with a parochial conscience in a universal world. This is the ultimate problem for the ecumenical movement, the problem which it simply must solve if it is to become conclusive and decisive, and so to advance.

For the implication of this is that public opinion in the churches continues to be attached to attitudes and behaviour patterns which hinder the perception of what needs to be perceived today, and prevent what should happen from happening. We still divide the world into 'us' and 'them'. We still think of 'peace' as 'law and order' instead of seeing it as an open-ended process in which conflicts are resolved in love and hope. Submissiveness is still considered more Christian than resistance, lacking as we do criteria for the unity of these two virtues. The *status quo* is still given higher religious value than change. To cross the frontiers in dialogue, by cooperation, by showing interest in the identity of another, by being concerned at another's sufferings — these are still regarded as endangering one's own 'deepest roots', even at a time when the frontiers are plainly melting away. For the conscience, 'foreign', 'hostile', and 'tabu' are synonyms. The organization of religious protest on an international scale is not easy in such an archaic pattern of piety. The Christianity of Christians is still trapped in the disabling symbiosis of religion and morality in which it formerly lived and operated meaningfully.

The needed transformation of public opinion, the 'forward leap' of the Christian conscience into a world outlook, cannot take place either, therefore. And still more far-reaching changes in church structures depend on this forward leap. Such changes do not depend solely on the goodwill or otherwise of church authorities. Church structures, whatever else they may be, are embodiments of dominant religious needs; a compromise between mandate and need. Only when a changed need is reflected in a noticeable shift in public opinion can structures themselves be modified beyond the permissible degree of purely cosmetic adjustments. And, since the decisiveness of the ecumenical movement depends on the member churches themselves overcoming their present indecisiveness as to how far changes can be permitted, the circle closes. The success or failure of the ecumenical movement will be decided by whether or not the parochial captivity of the Christian conscience can be ended.

It almost seems as if the struggle today is being waged on the wrong front. The ecumenical movement suffers because of the member churches. The member churches suffer because of the ecumenical movement. This seems to suggest that a power struggle is going on between two levels of church initiative and competence. Without the support of ordinary Christians, however, both levels are incompetent. They both stand or fall with the liberation of the parochial conscience. Any strategy to meet this situation will have to be a joint educational strategy on the part of the World Council and its member churches: a joint strategy for educating the church membership. I do *not* mean the manipulation of church members by propaganda. I mean the development of their capacity to make decisions. Both the New Delhi formula and the conciliarity formula come to a sharp focus here: how capable are Christians of active reception?

The World Council of Churches had — belatedly — added to its range of activities a desk on education. At present it is almost exclusively concerned with questions relating to the world crisis in education and with the Church's responsibilities in the educational 'class society' which seems to be developing. That is entirely as it should be, since the educational situation in society is also the context of all domestic church educational programmes. Yet the logic of the ecumenical process seems to point the new office of education ultimately in quite a different direction. The question to which it needs to find an answer is how Christians can grow so as to continue to be adequate for the world in which they are called to believe, to love and to hope.

4. Why the Time is Short

People are irresolute, undecided. The churches are also irresolute and undecided, therefore. And while they remain so, the ecumenical movement remains inconclusive.

Play is splendid. Play is a vital part of life. But we can spend too much time in play. We can throw away our opportunity.

The ecumenical movement is undoubtedly the most promising enterprise of Christendom in our time, perhaps even the most promising enterprise of mankind in this era of interdependence. But we must be under no illusions. Apart from the international cooperation between the churches, the only other irrevocable thing that has happened is this: A very complex, astonishingly neat and flexible 'agreement to disagree' has been achieved. A common ecumenical negotiating language has been invented, a common stock of words and phrases in which each of the participants can accommodate his faith and his doubts, his experience and his limitations, his hope and his resistance. But everyone knows that the same words are being used to express quite different things, knows that there are overtones and things left unexpressed, the emotions and the dreams, whose compatibility has still to be put to the test.

We know from the political field that even to find a common working language is a considerable achievement. The nations have not yet come even within hailing distance of such an achievement.

Serious discussions could, therefore, now begin; a start could be made on common action, action as a *united* fellowship and not just *ad hoc* cooperation. Only in the process of

negotiation and common action of this kind will the words
and the phrases become unequivocal.

The difficulty lies in the fact that, at another level, in a
different dimension, the ecumenical movement is already
much further on. Because, as I have said, the unequivocal
words are not yet available, it is difficult to offer any precise
description of this wide margin between ecumenical realities,
on the one hand, and ecumenical language, ecumenical
theory and ecumenical praxis, on the other. It is not hard to
find metaphors and analogies. When a man and a woman are
making their promises before the registrar, promises which
will alter the very quality of their relationship, they will still
have the awareness and the habits of single people. In reality
they are already much further on than that, but they will need
time to feel their way into the new relationship and to become
accustomed to it.

But comparisons are lame. The real ecumenical situation is
that although the member churches are irresolute, afraid to
take the irrevocable step out of disunity because they are still
not sure of the peace this will bring, they also know that this
reaction is not only no longer a proper one, but even untrue
and disobedient, and this for three reasons.

It is untrue and disobedient, firstly, in face of our common
origin. This has now been so thoroughly explored that it has
ceased to be merely a general truth known to all but binding
on none and become a concrete obligation.

It is untrue and disobedient, secondly, in face of a future
which certainly can only be our common future. By this I
mean not the eschatological future but the historical future,
the future many of whose contours are even now discernible.
There is no longer any future for our divided churches. There
are massive reasons for this: the growth of the world's
population, compelling economic and international political
pressures, the growing disproportion between task and
resources, between increasing obligations and diminishing
effectiveness in educational and health services, in theological
research, and so on.

Even more important is the fact that the churches, having
allowed themselves the ecumenical possibility, even if only 'on
approval' and not realizing its implications, are now subject
to a 'growth pressure'. Even for the individual, retreat is often

enough fatal, in the end. Societies disintegrate when they succumb to the temptation to retreat: fascism, isolationism, fundamentalism are illustrations of this. And this is especially true of religious institutions with their peculiarly emotional relationship to the truth. To suppress a problem after it has once consciously presented itself, to flee from a horizon once it has been revealed, results in sterility, impotence, and this in many ways. The truth once known turns into a lie when, having seen its wider context, one closes one's eyes to this wider truth out of fear or irresolution.

Persistence in division is untrue and disobedient, thirdly, because the world around the churches, people inside and outside the churches, who are looking for certainty, no longer accept division in the old sense. Their consciences may be parochial, but they nevertheless no longer comprehend this division. For what the churches allege to be divisive, they no longer have either the words or the experience. But they see other divisions even in the churches and between them, which are not confessional in character. How far this collapse of the possibilities of comprehension has carried can be seen at such sensitive points as the problem of mixed marriages, denominational educational policies, a whole series of controversial issues of social ethics, where people are quite simply incapable of seeing any necessary connection between these problems and basic dogmatic decisions.

In the eyes of this world around them, churches which spend so much time and money on regulating inter-church relationships while the number of people in the world who are starved of bread, meaning and justice is growing day by day are incredible churches. So far as human expectations are concerned, something which might be called the *one* Christendom has long existed, though chiefly as a disappointed expectation. But this dangerous consensus of disappointed hopes is something which the churches in the long run cannot ignore. For it is a symptom of a decay in the indigenous character of the churches, an erosion of their presence and competence in the world in which they live.

The opposite is even more conclusive. Whenever experimental groups and institutions venture a pathfinding sortie towards that horizon of expectation, it is almost invariably an ecumenical venture or else it fails. In the ghettos of the great cities, where unqualified solidarity is the order of the day, not even the heavily guarded frontier between Rome and the non-Roman churches can still remain inviolate.

Wherever the world still feels, or feels again, the need for Christendom, it is the *one* Christendom it needs, or else feels betrayed by the *one* Christendom.

The upshot of all this is that the churches do not have unlimited time to overcome their ecumenical irresolution. This means that the ecumenical movement itself must reckon with wear and tear. Expectations cannot be persisted in indefinitely. Revolutionary sensitivity soon grows old and tired. Neither individuals nor institutions can live on credit indefinitely. And the ecumenical movement can be described as the way the churches are living on credit today.

This credit can run out. Of course, interchurch aid and ecumenical development aid to the world will continue. But the surplus, the extra quality, hidden in the laboriously achieved bridge formulas, in common statements, in the common insights and plans, in forms of joint cooperation and organization, this could sink without trace. For the young ecumenical *avant-garde* it already has. For the small section of the church membership which has long been ecumenically awake (in the USA, for example), it has already strained to breaking point while the majority remains almost untouched by it. The pioneers have passed on. The technocrats of the second and third generations have much less vivid dreams and are easily tempted to settle for the short-term possibilities.

Here, if anywhere, it really is true that stagnation is dangerous. Retreat is no longer a possibility. The call to advance has become imperative and inescapable.

The Test Case of Faith

Dear Friend,

I recall writing a letter to the General Secretary of the World Council of Churches shortly before taking up my post in Geneva and still find myself rather embarrassed when I think of the grand words I used in it. I was at pains to explain my real motive for making the change to Geneva. What I said was: 'I want to do something for peace'. I know now that such things, which sound a little ridiculous, not least to oneself, are better left unsaid.

However, as an implicit assessment of the churches' ecumenical enterprise, I do not feel that I really have to revise that statement. The ecumenical movement *is* a movement for peace. Far wider than the Geneva association, it is in fact the way in which the Christian churches really serve the cause of peace.

But this means that it is the way in which the churches today are truly churches. For the peace, the *shalom* proclaimed, exemplified and created in Jesus of Nazareth is the sole *raison d'être* of faith in him as Christ and of the social forms of this faith: it is its source and foundation, its driving force, mandate and purpose. Whatever else it may be, a church which ceases to understand itself in terms of *shalom*, which ceases to make *shalom* its focus, is not church but non-church. But if *shalom* can only be understood ecumenically, then ecumenical commitment at once becomes a criterion of the authenticity of the Church's existence today.

It is no longer possible to mince our words. For far too long ecumenical commitment has been simply one option among many for the local churches, a matter of indifference, one area of activity among others. Ecumenism can no longer be toyed

147

with as a mere possibility. It has become the test case of faith. Today there is only one way of putting the four credal marks of the Church into practice, only one way for the Church to be one, holy, catholic and apostolic, and that is the ecumenical way. And being ecumenical is at the same time the contemporary expression of peace, of *shalom*.

I

'To speak is to love', says an African proverb. The problem is that, in all the choices confronting us in organizing peace, this statement can be, and indeed must be, reversed, if we are to understand fully the extent to which there is a 'deficit' of peace. The parley is a demonstration of love amid the conflict of needs and interests. This means, however, that love is always an essential prerequisite. Only those who love will continue to insist that discussions must go on. Only those who hope will insist on continuing the parley. Only those who invest faith in the parley will be vindicated.

Faith, love, hope — the three driving forces of the Christian life — seem in some way to be essential prerequisites for the organizing of peace. Does this not make the organization of peace a utopian enterprise in the bad sense of the word? Does it not inevitably rank it with all the other hopelessly utopian plans which demand too much of men? Good relationships create good human beings, but who creates the good relationships?

This is the crucial aspect of the 'deficit' of peace which is of such decisive importance for man's future. For what is here required is a leap forward in human development, an ethical mutation.

This can be put in quite specific terms. Man has no inhibition about killing his fellowmen, at least none that works instinctively. In this respect, he is not controlled by his instincts but must, on the contrary, learn to control them. He has to make good his deficiency in this respect by creating institutions.

The previous course of human history shows, moreover, that this solution is a feasible one, that man *can* institutionalize his life. The reluctance to kill may not be instinctive but it can be instilled into him, and indeed has been learned and can be more or less depended on in all established groups. A parent rarely kills his offspring although there are infanticidal tendencies in every one of us. In all societies murder is a crime, at least within the limits of that particular group. Yet it is also undeniable that this rule has only operated effectively in history so far when man's aggressive tendencies could be directed to some object outside the group.

But that immediately poses the question: Does it always have to stay that way? Is this a permanent feature of human nature? Must we be free to murder strangers in order to be able to tolerate our kith and kin? To put it another way: must the fifth commandment be made into a universal one, and in its strictest interpretation, as found for example in the Sermon on the Mount, since otherwise it makes no sense? Thou shalt not take another person's life but, on the contrary, find room and time for his life in your own, for only then will you yourself really live! Is that a feasible minimum requirement for membership of the human race?

Whatever the answer, what is certain is that if the answer is no, then peace, too, is impossible. Only when it is no longer possible to break off the parley and murder your partner, can there be any chance of peace as a world-wide palaver, as a universal conclave from which no one emerges until agreement has been reached. This is precisely what is meant when we say that peace is the crucial 'deficit' for the future of mankind. Man is a being in transit who will either achieve *this* transition to a universal morality based on the fifth commandment, as he has also achieved other moral advances in his historical evolution, or else perish. Peace is the programme for mankind on which the very survival of the species and its human evolution depend.

II

The problem of peace, therefore, constitutes the inescapable context which determines the relevance and credibility of Christianity and its social expression today. A Christianity which cannot relate itself to mankind's increasingly urgent need for peace is irrelevant. It lacks the very minimum of credibility required for communication of any kind. The theme of peace stands on the agenda. The

Church can reformulate it, expand it, examine it critically in different contexts, but either it addresses itself to the theme or it has nothing whatever to say.

This is precisely why ecumenical commitment is a criterion of the authenticity of the Church's life today. For the theme is universal peace. And ecumenism is the form, the only form, in which the universality of Christianity is possible today. In the one world, Christianity is present ecumenically — or not at all. This still leaves open the question of how this presence is expressed. Even if there were no ecumenical movement, no World Council of Churches, the existence of the one world would still be a challenge to the churches, a challenge to their ecumenical calling. Even for the individual local congregations the truth is that the ultimate frame of reference for their preaching, their service and the forms in which their church life finds expression, is world peace as the indispensable condition for a genuinely human future for mankind.

Nor is peace a theme which is foreign to the Christian community. It is indeed its own original theme. Rightly understood, it is the primary theme and the ultimate theme of faith. It is the message which in the ministry of Jesus engenders faith. And it is also the message which at the final judgement will vindicate faith on its own terms. Faith must necessarily be much more at home in this world where the absence of peace is so decisive for the future than in any of the parochial worlds from which it comes, where the chief concern was always the survival of one group at the expense of others.

The provoking thing is that Christianity has a way of speaking of peace which is different from that of the world of nations: a way which is at once more elementary and more utopian. It is not, of course, speaking of a different peace. The *shalom* proclaimed and exhibited in the tradition of the Christian faith is precisely the peace which other men have in mind: a life safe from, no longer threatened by the disaster of universal self-destruction; a new social life-style in which each accords others the room and the time to live; a new order with the fifth commandment as the golden rule of common life. The greatest hymn of peace in the Old Testament, Psalm 85, is unquestionably about earthly peace, and its interpretation and fulfilment in the life and ministry of Jesus is undoubtedly about life in this world.

Yet the churches' way of speaking of this same peace differs from that of the nations. The churches speak of it as a peace which has already been given, a *datum*, and, at the same time, as an eschatological promise, as the future of futures. According to Christian faith, there is a divine credit-balance of peace, guaranteed both by the past and by the future, more than sufficient to offset mankind's deficit.

In my own view, this twofold provocation to all political efforts for peace in our contemporary world (political in the broadest sense of the term) is quite indispensable. If it did not already exist, it would have to be invented. It is more than ever essential now that mankind can no longer rely as a matter of course on existing, tried and tested systems in his efforts to shape his world. Now it is up to him to produce his own plans for the future.

The rational plan has replaced the sacrosanct order as man's guide to the ordering of his common life. Reduced to its starkest terms, this is the mutation which has taken place in human evolution. But the threat to human life is thereby intensified. The sacrosanct order was at least based on past experience. To be prisoners of ossified traditions may have been bad enough. But the threatened imprisonment in the plans and programmes, the dreams and world schemes which the political calculators and prophets are devising, will certainly be far worse. For these plans have still to be put to the test. And the more all-embracing the project is, the greater the risk of putting its feasibility to the test, since in the last analysis this means irretrievably putting it into practice.

A clear illustration of the ambivalence of directing human existence by social planning is the vision of the classless society which today already captures the imagination of nearly two-thirds of mankind. This project cannot be evaded, for two reasons: in the first place, it is the most outstanding and clear-cut of the options open to mankind today and, in the second place, it is also a recipe for political action which clearly comes closer to the longings of the great majority of human societies — with the exception, for the moment at least, of the highly industrialized, former colonial Atlantic nations — than any of the bourgeois world-schemes, whose indecision in face of the present problem of mankind's survival becomes more and more obvious. But the very attractiveness and popularity of this vision tempts it to make absolute claims and to take on a quasi-religious aura, to become not so much a provisional plan subject to revision as rather a universal recipe, a complete solution for all mankind's problems, claiming the total allegiance of its devotees, their total sacrifice and total identification. But the more totalitarian it becomes, the more 'eschatological' it becomes, too — a description of what is radically beyond our reach — and the less it offers in the way of practical guidance, the more it overtaxes its adherents, the more it ruthlessly sacrifices today's happiness and freedom for tomorrow's, the more it creates frustration, the more it irrationally evades criticism in the light of the facts, and the more firmly entrenched become the early phases of the revolution, the supposedly temporary dictatorial arrangements, as necessary guarantees of the coming order.

But we should harbour no illusions. The classless society may be the most outstanding of man's visions of peace and for that very reason the most vulnerable and the one most in need of critical scrutiny. But even the more modest, less radical goals — reformist capitalism, for example, or nationalist liberation programmes in the Third World — are also visions and the same danger of absolutism is present in them all. Even the counter-proposals of the conservatives — the 'law and order' concept, or the 'defensive programme' of the fascists, the isolationists and the political fundamentalists — are unmistakably visions, too. They do not really defend tried and tested assets and healthy systems which only need to be maintained and developed, despite their claims to do so. Their plans, too, are fabrications, however much they may seem to follow the traditional blueprints. And at bottom, they are far more utopian than the visions of the Left, for they ignore or cover up the real extent of the decay in the previous systems. Reinstatement is certainly more utopian, in the bad sense, than innovation. Neither the 'Right' nor the 'Left' can escape the historic destiny which makes contemporary man responsible for envisioning his own future.

Hence the absolute necessity of the twofold protest against the assumption that man's future is *entirely* within his own power to programme. This twofold protest is one which the churches raise and represent, or *could* represent if they took the 'deficit' of peace as the fundamental frame of reference for their witness today. The churches have to maintain two positions here:

Firstly, they have to set against all human visions, the divine vision, i.e. perfect peace, *shalom*. To the extent that they manage to do so, they offer vital resistance to the tendency of all human visions to transform themselves into universal utopias, and to set themselves above criticism and correction. In a world which depends on visions, higher courts of appeal are needed to cut human visions down to size and to keep them open and flexible. Where this does not happen, hope dies and, with it, the dynamic of all visions. *Shalom* is God's vision for mankind and radically transcends all conceivable human programmes. It is the ultimate promise which makes all human plans penultimate and therefore malleable. It is the custodian of the inexhaustibility of hope.

As custodian of the vision of the resurrection and eternal life, a vision which is as absurd as it is inescapable, it counters the deep pessimism underlying even the most radical of human projects, the fatalistic acceptance of death as the most certain fact about life.

As custodian of the vision of the eschatological reversal of all earthly conditions, when God's strength will be made perfect precisely in the weak, the sick, the handicapped, it counters all the various ways of disregarding death — the worship of youth, vitality, health, achievement, strength and intellect — which are the mirror-image of fatalistic pessimism.

As custodian of the threat of final judgement, the warning that we shall all ultimately be called to account for all our deeds, it counters the Promethean arrogance of man as he discovers himself to be his own maker (*faber sui*) and imagines that all things are now possible to him and, because possible, therefore justifiable.

As custodian of the religious assurance of the *apokatastasis panton* (universal salvation), of the conviction that all ways — even the unending uphill way of Sisyphus — must ultimately lead to the goal, a conviction to which it must cling if it is to continue to believe that God is God, even though it cannot

even presume to speak of it in reference to itself, it counters
the melancholy Sisyphean fatalism which is convinced by
bitter experience that the goal is for ever unattainable and
which is no longer able, therefore, to summon up the courage
to even work towards a goal.

As custodian of the infinite value of the individual life, of
individual suffering and personal sorrow, in the sight of God,
it counters the tacit or deliberate betrayal of the individual to
the collective, a betrayal which lurks in every human project.

And as custodian of the vision of the new covenant in which
every one deals justly with his fellows, it counters the fatal
tendency of all individuals to achieve their own happiness at
the expense of the happiness of some or all the others and by
isolating themselves from the collective.

What it has custody of, in all the richness of this promise of
the kingdom, is the hope of perfection. Without this hope,
man cannot live, cannot bear even the obvious imperfection of
his visions and what becomes of them in practice. From this
hope springs the strength to criticize and to be self-critical, the
strength to go on beginning afresh. In other words, if he
cannot hold open this indispensable hope of perfection, if he is
not permitted to trust God for its fulfilment, he finds
unbearable the thought that imperfection is inevitable and the
inevitable imperfect. Lacking the hope of perfection, he
cannot find the precarious balance between resistance and
submission on which his survival and his human development
depend.

It would be a mistake for Christians to abandon the
richness of this hope of the kingdom simply because the
traditional images in which it has been expressed present
serious language problems. What is called for today is neither
that we should squander the eschatological credit-balance,
dramatizing the contemporary decision of faith as if all
eternity were to be found in the 'today' of human
introspection, nor that we should reduce it to the measure of
what can be achieved by Christian activism. Theologians
must, rather, stretch their imaginations in the search for new
ways of speaking of this eschatological 'fortune' which, while
keeping its richness intact, at the same time relate it to man's
projects for peace. Christians have no right to proclaim
anything short of the kingdom, since anything short of the

kingdom falls legitimately within the scope of man's own planning and action.

It cannot be assumed that the churches will be accepted in this critical role by the secular world as they were in the Constantinian era when the parochial human orders were firmly moored in the *ordo Dei* by the Church. The relation between human peace projects and the proclamation of the kingdom of God is far more tense than that between *ordo* and order. In societies which must concentrate all their efforts on peace projects, churches which relativize these projects by their every word and deed, by their very existence even, will be considered as, literally, 'disturbers of the peace'. Nor will the old strategy of coalitions serve any longer to mitigate the inevitable conflict between the builders of peace on earth and the heralds of the kingdom of God. The relationship between the Soviet State and its churches, with its pattern of unobtrusive yet constant struggle, provides a better preview of what is in store than the camaraderie between Nixon and Billy Graham.

The churches' eschatological protest against all totalitarian pretensions in social planning is not a conflict between religious idealism and revolutionary action. For the images of the kingdom extrapolate an historical process, the pro-cess of Jesus, the pro-cess of Israel which culminates in Jesus. To the Christian, *shalom* is not just the unattainable horizon of all rational human projects but also their permanent pre-supposition and pattern. The vision of peace is rooted in history as well as in eschatology. This is why the churches so stubbornly persist in maintaining that the *shalom* of God surpasses all rational goals (Phil. 4:7). They are able to point to the concrete historical instance of a life actually lived on the basis of this inexhaustible eschatological 'fortune'.

Obviously Jesus Christ is not the only relevant example for mankind in its quest for peace and human development. For Christians he is, in any case, more than an example, much more. Christians confess him as the One who, precisely because he is 'very God', is also 'very man'. In other words, he is the eschatological fullness in person. For Christians, he is quite simply the new man, eschatological man, man in his fulfilment. This is still disputed. But it is tremendously important that humanity, saddled as it is with the task of

programming itself, should also be continually confronted not
only with its inexhaustible eschatological future but also with
the inexhaustible credit-balance of its past. We have much to
do, but we are not set the task of re-inventing humanity from
scratch. What humanity is has already been decided and
historically documented in an unsurpassable way. Jesus
cannot, of course, be impersonated. The proclamation of the
new humanity in him does not relieve us of the responsibility
of programming our future. But, in a quite specific sense,
Jesus' way of life is the criterion for every life-style devised by
men now and in the future. And this is so precisely because
his is not meant to be reproduced but rather to be constantly
adapted to changing conditions and itself provides, at the
same time, the incentive and the power to achieve such
adaptations. It does not lay down strict rules for human
praxis but guides it and judges it. It offers certain guiding
principles by which each historical situation is to be
relativized and set in movement. It makes extrapolations
possible.

One such permanent directive for human development, for
example, is the orientation of the ministry of Jesus towards
the margins of society. Sinners, lepers, demoniacs, Gentiles,
enemies — all those whom society expels to the margins, is
driven to expel to the margins for the sake of its own stability
— are embraced within the community of Jesus' love. More
precisely, his love in its transcendence reaches them where
they are. This transcendence, this inclusiveness, this bias to
universality, is the very essence of love.

Another directive provided by the praxis of Jesus is the
advance from lordship to service, from paternalism to
fraternity, from subjection to liberation. In Jesus' way of life,
the lowest is highest, is given priority, exercises power, has an
authority which is not inherent but conferred on it by faith.

A third directive is the movement of Jesus from the sacred
to the profane. The division of the world into holy and unholy
spheres, into places close to God and places shut off from him,
disappears. The whole of reality is rich with promise, and this
axiom militates against all man's repeated attempts to split
the world into the sacred and the profane.

A fourth pointer, already implicit in the previous one, is the
biased way in which Jesus insists, not on judging life's

possibilities in the light of what is, but what is in the light of its eschatological possibilities, in the light of the promise. That is why the excluded must be brought into the community, why the power of the powerless must be respected, why the holiness of the 'profane' must be reckoned with.

These few examples must suffice. They at least suggest how Jesus' programme for his own life can become the pattern, the criterion and incentive for future programmes. Yet it should be remembered that, in this respect, Jesus of Nazareth is more than simply a historical figure. His handling of life became in the first place the key to Israel's history and to its unique significance. It then became the touchstone for the history of the Church and of Christianity, for all that is of permanent value in that history and still significant for the future. And finally, it has become custodian of the permanent gains of mankind's past history in its entirety. It spotlights what is of abiding significance, what is worth keeping. For example, in the light of the life Jesus lived, it is clear that the reverence for all life is an enduring value in Hinduism, an advance in human development from which there can be no retreat.

But even as custodian of the permanent gains of man's past, the Church will not win the undisturbed friendship of a world preoccupied with its hopes and plans for peace. Both as pattern and key to tradition, Jesus is a disturbing factor. Even in the period of the Constantinian coalition he was uncommonly disturbing.

Yet it is precisely by being an irritant, a built-in protest, a witness to the 'unsearchable riches of Christ', precisely as the presence and action of the non-contemporary, of that which is still to come and of that which is past, and only in this way, that the social forms of Christianity can find a truly indispensable place in mankind's peace programme.

III

You may say that all this is a highly subjective and rather questionable account of the contribution Christianity could make to the coming world community. But what on earth has it got to do with the ecumenical movement and with ecumenism as the criterion of authentic church life today?

The answer is that the Church cannot fulfil its role as custodian of the 'unsearchable riches' of Christ merely by words alone. From the very beginning, the transmission of the Christian faith and experience has depended on there being some sponsor, some guarantor, a living and institutional sponsor and guarantor, of that faith and experience. Jesus himself — in person — is the guarantor of the new way of life which he expects of and entrusts to his contemporaries. On the strength of his word, his person, his presence, his ministry, people began to believe, to love, to hope. 'No man has ever seen God', declares John. 'But God's only son, he who is nearest to the Father's heart, has made him known' (Jn. 1:18). The man from Nazareth is the guarantor of that which even in the New Testament is inconceivable and inexpressible. On the strength of the surety provided by Jesus, men begin to live *etsi Deus daretur*.

That continues to be the wellspring of faith. Only this surety enables us to enter on the way of life along which God grants us experience of himself. And as we begin the life of faith in this way, so we ourselves in turn stand surety for others. The way we actually live must commend God, if others are to speak of God and put their trust in him. There is nothing specifically religious about this. In every area of human life we depend on others standing surety for us and others on us standing surety for them. The presence of guarantors is the secret of all traditions and all movements of renewal, of all educational and liberation processes.

It is also the deepest reason why Christianity must, in all circumstances, assume a social form, whether by forming churches or in other ways. Human life in practice — and faith is nothing if it is not a way of life — is by definition life in society. It is therefore a life which depends on order. The Church is the network of interlocking sponsorship relations which provides access to faith as a way of life and makes its transmission possible. The Church is the sponsoring society for the divine sponsorship in which faith believes and trusts. In it the individual Christian stands surety — together with the whole community — and the whole community stands surety — together with all its individual members — for the credit-worthiness of God. In it the strong stand surety for the weak and the weak for the strong, the old for the young and the young for the old. They do so, moreover, in quite concrete ways wherever the believing way of life is 'threatened', i.e. wherever it breaks down, wherever it seems in danger of breaking down under the pressure of godless forces. Since even the strong are not exempt from the possibility of becoming weak, they need the weak as guarantor. And the weak need the surety that the strong can provide, so that they, too, may learn the strength promised also to them. In the Church, the individual congregation stands surety for the whole institution, and the whole institution for the individual congregation; the people of God for its ministers and the ministers for the whole people of God; theology for piety and piety for theology.

Above all, by its proclamation, action and order, the Church is the guarantor of faith for the world around it. And even between Church and world, there is a reciprocal relationship. In a real sense the world around the Church also stands surety for the credit-worthiness of God, since faith also depends on being able again and again to discern the truth of God shining forth in the world.

'Standing surety', therefore, is the instrumentality of God's presence in his world. It has here strictly the same sense as it has in its economic use. The person or group which guarantees the credit-worthiness of another person or group makes business transactions possible, makes credit possible. The double sense of the term 'credit' is not just a play on words, therefore.

To describe the Church as a complex network of interrelated guarantees is far more than a merely formal description. The Church stands surety for Jesus, who stands surety for God; it stands surety for a quite specific way of life which commends God. Only what is consistent with that way of life can be an effective and responsible guarantee. Conformity with Jesus' way of life is therefore the criterion of authentic church life and being. For obvious historical and theological reasons, this conformity can never be more than the congruence of the incongruous, a relationship which is essentially a convincing or unconvincing appeal to authority. All the same, the discovery that the fundamental structure of the Church is this network of interrelated guarantees clearly exposes the inadequacy, for example, of the Lutheran concept of the Church, at least as represented by the traditional understanding of chapter VII of the Augsburg Confession. The Church stands surety for Jesus both by its faith *and* by its order. To that extent the objections of the 'catholic' churches to Protestant church structures are justified. But, taken seriously, these objections recoil at once upon these churches themselves. In what sense do the authoritarian religious systems of hierarchically ordered churches conform to the movement — so fundamental in Jesus' way of life — from domination to service, from paternalism to fraternity, from subjection to liberation?

If the Church is faith's guarantor, especially in concrete situations where faith finds itself assailed, when the language of facts gives the lie to God, it is not difficult to see why ecumenism is the contemporary criterion for an authentic churchmanship and why the ecumenical movement is indispensable for the churches. In a world whose entire future is indissolubly linked with the problem of the deficit of universal peace and in its dealings with a human race driven to efforts to achieve universal peace by the threat of disaster, the Church is summoned to stand surety for the *shalom* of God and this it can only do ecumenically: by incorporating in the community those who have been relegated to the margins, by putting the powerless into power, by sanctifying the profane, by anticipating here and now what has been promised.

Ecumenism has a very precise connotation. Mankind is threatened by its failure so far to come to terms with political, economic, social, and cultural interdependence on a world scale. The choice is between an international community of law and order or disaster. The now bogus division of mankind into various species, into groups, races, nations, though it may once have enabled mankind to survive, has become a deadly menace. In this situation, the challenge which the churches cannot evade is to stand surety for man's capacity to move forward to a new situation. They must show that in Christ the divisions of mankind become opportunities for charismatic cooperation, concrete examples of unity, occasions for consensus (Gal. 3:28). In a situation in which the confession of faith is literally 'shouted down' by the language of facts, by uncontrolled interdependence, what the churches must stand surety for — in their doctrine and their order and their political *diakonia* (what other kind of *diakonia* is there other than one which serves in the life of the *polis*?) — is precisely *shalom* as the conciliar reconciliation of the irreconcilable. Ecumenism is certainly *more* than internationalism. But it does include internationalism. And today, when the whole future of mankind depends on the achievement of an effective international order of justice and peace, it is more than ever a question of internationalism. Anything else is sheer humbug. Churches which are incapable of crossing the traditional frontiers, churches which are perhaps not even aware of the relevance of faith's bias towards the frontiers, are fated to become unauthentic churches, no longer the irritant which is absolutely vital for mankind's advance towards peace.

But failure to achieve an international order of justice and peace is not the only evidence of inability to deal with our inescapable interdependence. There is also the constant ironing-out of individuality, the constant erosion of personal and group identities in our Coca-Cola world. Mankind is not only failing with its international future, it is even letting the richness and variety of its past slip through its fingers. And the two things are connected. If the Church is to stand surety in this situation, it means that it must be committed more than ever before — precisely as a universal conciliar organization — to the particular, the local, the individual, to champion identities, and to do this, too, in its faith *and* its order, *and* in its political *diakonia*. This is the other side of the coin of ecumenism, the ecumenism needed today. It is *not* uniformity. That is one of the oldest insights of the ecumenical movement. That the churches had to be taught the thousand and one variations of the maxim 'black is beautiful'; that the churches did not discover this for themselves despite the fact that it is an implicitly Christian truth; that the churches should feel themselves threatened by ground-level ecumenism with its concern for and solidarity with oppressed minorities and by the 'underground' churches which have sprung up all over the world, instead of providing these protest movements with room and time and opportunity to take part in world-wide conciliar exchange, representing as they do the churches' responsibility to stand surety at a most fundamental level; that the request to the churches to halt their missions to dying cultures in Latin America and elsewhere because these traditional missions are inexorably helping to complete the destruction of these cultures should have had to come from concerned ethnologists; — all these facts constitute as severe an indictment of the churches as they at present exist as it is possible to imagine.

Only by ecumenical action, only by uniting the incompatible, only by demonstrating the art of faith, which champions the universal rights of the particular and stands surety for concrete universality, for an international, intercultural consensus, will the churches make credible amends for their betrayal of the universal (parochialism) and of the particular (their cult of conformity).

IV

Even by their ecumenical obedience, the churches do not relieve mankind of its responsibility for programming peace. The churches stand surety for the same peace which mankind is seeking but do so in a quite special way. They are 'disturbers of the peace', witnesses to the alpha and the omega of peace, and as such they make all human projects for peace relative. The international order of justice and peace on which mankind's future depends cannot be achieved in accordance with the ecumenical model, even if the churches themselves take this model seriously.

Yet individuals and groups do provide examples of ecumenical action: religious organizations working at every level of social action, displaying an immense variety of individual and corporate life-styles. We find them precisely in situations of human conflict where people are searching for peace. The presuppositions of the ecumenical programme may differ from those of society's hopes for peace but the programme has to be made a reality in and through the very same materials of secular world society.

To this extent, the ecumenical programme is an alternative to the world's peace plans. And alternatives are opportunities to learn. Churches which are working out their ecumenical destiny will certainly stimulate people's imagination as they work at their peace plans. They could, for example, do what the nations in their international efforts seem quite unable to do, namely, ensure full equality between the unequal, between strong and weak, between rich and poor, in all the decision-making processes. This is obviously still not the case in the World Council of Churches, but it is ecumenically conceivable, and even inescapable. The truer it becomes, the more it will bring pressure to bear on the relations between nations. There, of course, the equality of the unequal will undoubtedly take a very different form, but willy-nilly it will have to learn from the alternative offered by the churches. In the history of Christianity, the alternatives offered by active faith have repeatedly proved relevant in spite of distinctive assumptions and goals. In the measure that the churches quietly pursue their own objectives without always and everywhere having to assume the role of schoolmaster to the world and vanguard of mankind, in the measure that they exploit their own potential, the potential of faith, to that extent will they really become an institutionalized irritant to mankind's own efforts for peace, custodian of the 'unsearchable riches' of Christ, an anticipation of God's *shalom,* and also a stimulus to such efforts.

Well, that's my ecumenical testament! Knowing you know your Bible well, I can imagine you quoting the words of the Ethiopian eunuch: 'Tell me, please, *who* it is that the prophet is speaking about here?' Does he really mean the churches such as they are?

My answer: Yes, I mean the real churches — in the light of their possibility. I mean the real churches — under the pressure of their calling. This calling, I believe, obliges them to make the ecumenical utopia a reality. Of course, it is well known that the churches betray their calling.

Shalom!

Yours,

E.L.

Appendix

Conciliarity and the Future of the Ecumenical Movement

'The Uppsala Assembly spoke of the World Council as "a transitional opportunity for eventually actualizing a truly universal, ecumenical, conciliar form of common life" and suggested that the member churches should "work for the time when a genuinely universal council may once more speak for all Christians and lead the way into the future". Though related, these two suggestions need to be distinguished. The first points to a permanent feature of the Church's life, while the second refers to an event which may once take place. To accept the first suggestion of the Uppsala Assembly will mean that we seek to deepen the element of conciliarity in the life of the churches at all levels, local, regional and universal. The New Delhi statement on the nature of the unity we seek spoke of a "fully committed fellowship" both "in each place" and also universally, embracing the Church in all ages and places. To accept conciliarity as the direction in which we must move means deepening our mutual commitment at all levels. This does not mean movement in the direction of uniformity. On the contrary, our discussions here at Louvain have emphasized the fact that, if the unity of the Church is to serve the unity of mankind, it must provide room both for wide variety of forms and for differences and even conflicts. The conciliarity of the Church requires the involvement of the entire lay membership, including as it should every segment of mankind. There must be opportunity within the life of the Church for each community of mankind to develop and express its own authentic selfhood; for the oppressed and exploited to fight for justice; and for the "marginal" people in society — the handicapped in mind and body — to make their own distinctive contribution. This becomes all the more necessary because modern technology has forced all mankind into a tight interdependence which constantly threatens freedom and individuality. The Church's unity must be of such a kind that there is ample space for diversity and for the open mutual confrontation of differing interests and convictions.' (§4)

'True conciliarity, moreover, has a temporal dimension; it links the past, the present and the future in a single life. This is part of the meaning of what New Delhi said about the unity of the committed fellowship "in all ages and places". Through the work of the Spirit in the life of the Church, we are enabled to discern his teaching through the words of the Councils of the past. Within the living fellowship of the one Church we are enabled to enter into a conversation with the past, to put questions and to receive illumination on our own problems. We are not called upon simply to reproduce the words of the ancient Councils, which spoke to different situations and in languages other than ours. But it is an essential part of our growth into full conciliarity that we should be continually engaged in a process of "re-ception" of the Councils of the past, through whose witness — received in living dialogue — the same Holy Spirit who spoke to the Fathers in the past can lead us into His future.'(§5)

'In other words, certain of the elements of true conciliarity have begun to appear, even if only in a very preliminary way, in the life of the Council. The life of the member churches, and their relation to one another, have been significantly changed during the past two decades through their membership in the World Council of Churches. The ecumenical movement does move, even if the movement seems slow.' (§9)

'We suggest that it will be by strengthening these elements of true conciliarity in the life of the World Council of Churches and its member churches that we shall move

towards that "fully committed fellowship" of which the New
Delhi statement speaks. To accept this would mean at least
the following:

(*a*) that all the member churches seek more earnestly to
ensure that the ecumenical movement penetrates more and
more fully into the life of local congregations, synods and
assemblies of the churches;

(*b*) that member churches be encouraged to widen the area
of organic unity and of eucharistic fellowship among them,
wherever their fundamental ecclesiological principles permit;

(*c*) that the World Council of Churches explores still
further the ways in which it can provide fellowship, support
and guidance for those individuals and groups which are
seeking new forms of Christian obedience for which existing
ecclesiastical structures provide no opportunity;

(*d*) that the World Council be recognized as a place where
the great issues on which Christians are divided may be faced
— even at the risk of severe conflict, so that it may in a
measure fulfil the ancient function of a Council as a place
where Christians may be reconciled together in the truth;

(*e*) that member churches be encouraged to re-examine
and (when appropriate and possible) interpret anew their
polemical statements against each other;

(*f*) that the member churches together endeavour more
seriously to achieve unity in faith and to confess together our
hope for the world.' (§10)

(The full text from which these extracts are taken can be
found in *Louvain,* p. 225-229.)

Postscript

Since this book first appeared the work of the Faith and Order Commission has of course continued. The studies proposed at Louvain were initiated. New approaches have emerged. All this should be reported at least in broad outline. It has to be said at once, though, that Ernst Lange's observations on the basis of the Louvain documents have scarcely been invalidated by subsequent work. Indeed, reading his book five years later, one is astonished at the extent to which it already anticipated the Commission's present concerns. Lange's interpretation has so far stood the test of time. But just for this reason the reader may find it interesting to see how the themes proposed then have been dealt with since.

1. Consensus on Baptism, Eucharist and Ministry

The statements on baptism, eucharist and ministry presented to the Commission in Louvain were a first attempt to summarize the common convictions of the churches on these themes. The Commission accepted them and recommended that work on them should be continued. Ernst Lange saw at once the importance of this project. It was not simply a matter of producing an improved text but also, and above all, of discovering how this theological consensus could be received by the churches. What constitutes a real consensus? What form should the consensus take if it is really to contribute to unity? What changes are needed in the churches if the consensus is really to be assimilated by them?

Work was continued along these lines. Between Louvain and the next Commission meeting in Accra in 1974, the texts were thoroughly revised. But, at Accra, the Commission decided to halt temporarily the work of revision until the attitude of the churches to the results already achieved could be ascertained. The Fifth Assembly of the World Council of Churches in Nairobi accepted this proposal to submit the provisional statements to the member churches and asked for their comments to be sent in by December 31st 1976. About a hundred churches responded, and their replies were carefully evaluated by the Faith and Order commission. Its next task is to revise the statements in the light of these replies and to prepare a new version for presentation to the next Assembly.[30]

The momentous significance of this procedure is evident. Never before have the churches been so directly involved in the work of the Commission. The Accra decision was a practical expression of the conviction that our theological work must serve to unite the *churches* and that it must therefore be carried on in as close cooperation with the churches as possible.

It is interesting to notice that this immediately brought a number of fresh questions to the surface. If the new version of the consensus is to help the churches to make any progress towards unity, it will be necessary to explain what consensus really means. Once it is a question of establishing unity among the churches, a negative consensus no longer suffices. Positive agreed statements on baptism, eucharist and ministry are needed. Another question is how the churches can appropriate the consensus by mutually synchronized decisions. The decision of the Accra meeting to launch a study on the question 'How does the Church teach authoritatively today?' was not just coincidental. It obviously reflected the conviction that the churches must reach agreement on ways and means of joint reception, if they are to achieve one fellowship.

2. Unity of the Church and Unity of Mankind

The main theme of Louvain has continued to provide a special stimulus to ecumenical thinking since 1971. The conviction grew that the Faith and Order commission had to be concerned with the achievement of unity in the context of the contemporary world at least as much as with the solution of confessional differences. The Church must prove itself a reconciling element in human society. Its unity must be demonstrated above all wherever unity is threatened in human society. This conviction has been frequently expressed in a variety of ways, most clearly at the Nairobi Assembly.

The theological problems raised by the relation between Church and mankind were further explored at a consultation in which Ernst Lange himself participated. The report of this consultation used the terms 'sacrament' and 'sign' in an attempt to describe the Church's role within humanity. Through his presence, Christ makes the Church a sign in the world. By representing his presence sacramentally, the Church becomes the sign the endangered world needs. It becomes a sign for the world.[31]

But the stimulus of Louvain was not primarily at the general level of theological reflection. This reflection was left unfinished. In the years since Louvain it is rather to specific problems that the Commission has turned. What problems arise when the Church seeks to witness effectively to its unity in face of racial discrimination? What can it contribute to fellowship between man and woman? How can it become visibly a fellowship in which the handicapped have full scope to express themselves?

3. Conciliar Fellowship

Ernst Lange was undoubtedly right in his assessment of the importance of the Louvain statement on unity as conciliar fellowship. The Fifth Assembly in Nairobi not only considered the term but actually made it its own. To achieve this, a good many obstacles had first to be surmounted. For one thing, the Louvain statement had only been a draft. The vision of the one Church as a conciliar fellowship needed to be clarified further. It needed to be tested in the light of the ecclesiologies of the different confessional traditions. The Salamanca Consultation of 1973 had been an important stage in this process. It had provided a brief definition of 'conciliar fellowship', and this had been adopted first by the Commission in Accra and then by the Fifth Assembly in Nairobi.[32]

There is a certain tension between the Louvain statement, especially in Ernst Lange's interpretation of it, and the statement finally adopted in Nairobi. The concept of 'conciliar fellowship' was attractive to Ernst Lange primarily because it seemed to him to describe the Church as a fellowship which, while indeed one, is also constantly *becoming* one through the dynamic interplay of its many members. For him, conciliar fellowship was unity in diversity, unity in tension, even unity in conflict. He grasped here an important aspect of the concept, possibly the most important one. But he perhaps failed to notice sufficiently that the custodians of 'catholic' ecclesiologies could not share this interpretation as it stands.

This came out clearly in the course of discussion after Louvain. The conciliar fellowship is now understood, far more explicitly than at Louvain, as a continuation and restructuring of the unity given in Christ and in the tradition.

Since Louvain, the concept of 'conciliar fellowship' has also played an increasingly important part in the discussion of different 'methods of union', as Ernst Lange calls them. The proposal to take 'conciliar fellowship' as the goal of the ecumenical movement also raised the question of the relation between this model and others; for example, the 'organic union' model as envisaged in union negotiations, or the 'intercommunion in diversity' model used as a guiding principle in certain bilateral conversations. The Salmanca Consultation dealt with this aspect in some detail.

4.   Accounting for the Hope that is in Us

The proposal that we should seek a common expression of our common faith was accepted at Louvain only with a certain hesitation. The resistance came from two quarters. Firstly, there were those who considered that the Church's creed is something given to the Church which therefore cannot be made the subject of a new common formulation. Others were anxious lest the attempt to produce a common statement should lead to the suppression of certain important aspects of the diversity of the Church. What was needed was not an effort to produce common statements but rather to stress the rich variety of permissible expressions of the common faith.

Nevertheless, the study was undertaken. Two stages were planned. Firstly, the Commission invited the member churches to 'account for the hope' which sustains them in their own situations. Secondly, at a later stage in the study, it would be asked how far and in what way it was possible for the churches, despite the diversity of their views, to speak together of the common ground of their hope.

Participation in the study surpassed all expectations. A preliminary survey of the results was prepared at the Commission meeting in Accra in 1974.[33] The study is now entering the second stage. The question to which an answer must now be sought concerns the common ground (*logos*) of our hope. This brings us back once again, therefore, to the question already raised at Louvain. How can the common faith be confessed together? Clearly no immediately satisfactory answer is possible to this question. It raises a host of previous questions to which an answer must be found. Since Louvain, the Commission has conquered its hesitations and started work on the task presented by these questions.

Lukas Vischer

FOOTNOTES TO LANGE TRANSLATION

[1] Karl Marx, 'Introduction to *A Critique of Hegel's Philosophy of Right*', in *Early Texts*, ed. D. McLellan, Oxford 1971, p. 115.

[2] *Ecumenical Youth Assembly in Europe, Lausanne 1960*, published by the WCC Youth Department, Oct. 1960, No. 2.

[3] *World Conference on Church and Society*, Geneva 1966. Official Report with description of the Conference by M. M. Thomas and Paul Abrecht, WCC, Geneva, 1967.

[4] See *New Delhi Speaks*, SCM Press Ltd. 1962, the Report of the Third WCC Assembly. The phrase 'all in one place' is used and explained on p. 55 ff. in the report of the Section on Unity.

[5] See *op. cit.* n. 3 *supra*.

[6] Adapted from Walter Lowrie, *Kierkegaard*, Oxford University Press, London 1938, p. 544 f. See also Kierkegaard, *Journals 1853-1855*, Collins, Fontana Library, 1965, p. 292-3, Entry XI^2 A 210.

[7] The Faith and Order Commission is the present organization of one of the three main streams of the ecumenical movement which flowed into the World Council of Churches, first in 1948 and, in the case of the International Missionary Council, in 1961. The Commission's membership is restricted to 150 members, elected by the Assembly of the WCC with the approval of the churches from which they come. They include representatives of non-member churches 'who recognize Jesus Christ as God and Saviour'. Thus there are at present, for example, members of the Roman Catholic Church seated as members of the Commission. The Commission meets in full session every three years. A Working Committee is responsible for the work between sessions, assisted by the Geneva staff. The Geneva Secretariat is at present directed by Dr. Lukas Vischer.

[8]See By-Laws of the Faith and Order Commission, par. 2 'Aims and Functions', sect. (b). *Breaking Barriers, Nairobi 1975,* ed. D. Paton, SPCK, London & Wm. B. Eerdmans, Grand Rapids, p. 402.

[9]It was in 1920 that a preparatory conference was held in Geneva which eventually led to the First World Faith and Order Conference in Lausanne 1927. For the earlier history of Faith and Order see Tissington Tatlow's 'The World Conference of Faith and Order' in *A History of the Ecumenical Movement,* ed. Rouse and Neill, SPCK, London 1967, p. 405-441, and for the story after 1948, see *The Ecumenical Advance,* ed. Harold E. Fey, SPCK, London 1970, pp. 143 ff. 'Faith and Order 1948-1968' by Meredith B. Handspicker. A more popular account can be found in relevant chapters in Dr. Norman Goodall's two books: *The Ecumenical Movement,* OUP London 1961 and *Ecumenical Progress, A Decade of Change in the Ecumenical Movement 1961-1971,* OUP 1972.

[10]See *Fifty Years of Faith and Order,* Skogland and Nelson, New York, 1963, p. 19.

[11]More recently, the WCC was able to play an important part in preparatory work for a peace settlement in the Sudan. Practically nothing was heard of this, in contrast to the general outcry over the Programme to Combat Racism. Even the important part played by the Churches Commission on International Affairs (CCIA) and by leading Christian statesmen like Charles Malik of Lebanon in the negotiations which led up to the *Universal Declaration of Human Rights* is not generally known. See O. Frederick Nolde's essay on 'Ecumenical Action in International Affairs', in Harold E. Fey, *op. cit.* pp. 263 ff.

[12]Cf. the 'Call to the Churches', Geneva 1966, in the volume already referred to in n. 3 *supra.*

[13]Roman Catholicism, too, though a world Church, is indissolubly connected with a particular culture, namely that of Latin Europe. And even the small neo-pietistic groups of the North American and European revival movements and their missionary agencies were still expressions of a decided alliance with national 'ways of life'.

[14]See the chapters by Nils Karlström and Nils Ehrenström in Rouse and Neill, *op. cit.* p. 509 ff. and p. 545 ff. For the history of the Life and Work (Church and Society) movement since the founding of the WCC in 1948, sée Paul Abrecht's essay in Fey, *op. cit.* p. 233 ff.

[15]Short biographies of Brent and other founding fathers of Faith and Order can be found in Stephen C. Neill, *Men of Unity,* SCM Press Ltd. London, 1960.

[16]Skoglund and Nelson, *op. cit.* p. 14.

[17]Rouse and Neill, *op. cit.* p. 408.

[18]The expression appears in the report of an American study group in preparation for the Edinburgh Faith and Order Conference of 1937, 'The Non-Theological Factors in the Making and Unmaking of Church Union'. But it was not until Lund in 1952 that full attention was given to the problem.

[19]Even world conferences of Faith and Order, which are held by decision of the Central Committee of the WCC and are therefore WCC functions, can only 'bring to the attention of the churches, by the best means available, reports of Faith and Order meetings and studies', without in any way binding the churches even though these have been represented by official delegates who have shared in the work of the Assembly.

[20]Steven Mackie, *Patterns of Ministry,* Collins 1969.

[21]The fullest documentation on the controversy in Germany over the Programme to Combat Racism (PCR) was produced by Hans-Wolfgang

Hessler in collaboration with K. M. Beckmann in the Evangelical Press Service Documentation Series, No. 5, Witten-Berlin 1971. An assessment of the first five years of the PCR can be found in English in Elisabeth Adler, *A Small Beginning*, WCC Geneva 1974.

[22]See James H. Cone, *Black Theology and Black Power*, and more recently *God of the Oppressed*, Seabury Press Inc. 1975 and SPCK London 1977.

[23]See *The Human Studies, 1969-1975*, A collection of documents, ed. David Jenkins, WCC Geneva 1975.

[24]See report of this conference by David M. Gill, From here to where? Technology, faith and the future of man, Geneva WCC 1970.

[25]See Gill, *op. cit.* p. 85.

[26]See *Ecumenical Review*, Vol. XXIV 1972, p. 30-46.

[27]*Ibid.* pp. 47-50.

[28]W. Dantine, 'Systematische Erwägungen zum Studiendkument "Einheit der Kirche — Einheit der Menschheit"', in Una Sancta, Meitingen, Vol. 25 (1970), p.286-291.

[29]The author was probably quoting from memory here. Dr. Visser't Hooft in his *Memoirs* (SCM Press Ltd. London, Westminster Press Philadelphia, 1973) tells us that this conversation was with E. M. Robinson (p. 17).

[30]*One Baptism, One Eucharist and a Mutually Recognized Ministry*, Three Agreed Statements, Faith and Order Paper No. 73, WCC Geneva, 1975. *Towards an Ecumenical Consensus on Baptism, the Eucharist and the Ministry*, Faith and Order Paper No. 83, WCC Geneva 1977.

[31]*What Unity Requires*, Papers and Report on the Unity of the Church, Faith and Order Paper No. 77, p. 13.

[32]*What Unity Requires*, p. 14.

[33]*Minutes, Accra 1974*, Faith and Order Paper No. 71, WCC Geneva 1974. *Giving Account of the Hope That is Within Us*, WCC Geneva 1975.

NOTE ON WORKS CITED

Faith and Order, Louvain 1971, Study Reports and Documents, Faith and Order Paper No. 59, WCC Geneva 1971, cited as *Louvain*.

A Documentary History of the Faith and Order Movement 1927-1963, ed. Lukas Vischer, The Bethany Press, St. Louis, Missouri 1963, cited as *Doc. Hist.*

Commission on Faith and Order, *Minutes of the Meetings of the Working Committee and Commission, Louvain 1971*. Paper No. 60, WCC Geneva 1971, cited as *Minutes*.

Sources of all other quotations are indicated either in the text or in the footnotes.